Praise for Friends of Friends of Friends

Silver Medal in Relationships and Communication, Nautilus Awards
Silver Medal in Anthologies, Midwest Book Awards

"In this book of artfully crafted prose and photographs, Lee Fearnside and her contributors offer an antidote to the loneliness crisis. This book is a salve for our collective wounds." Dr. Allyson Day, author of The Political Economy of Stigma: HIV, Memoir, Medicine and Crip Positionalities (2021).

"Reading this book and those incredibly insightful and personal thoughts, it feels like community works like stories in inoculating against the forces and moments that force us apart, helping us find our way back, or at least prove a companion until we can." Matt Foss, co-writer and producer of the award-winning short film, Sons of Toledo (2021), named one of the Austin Film Festival and Movie Maker Magazine's Top 25 Screenwriters to Watch for 2023.

"For anyone interested in exploring the role of community in supporting change, reducing a loneliness epidemic, or living a good life, there is a lot to chew on here." Dr. W. John Koolage, Professor of Philosophy, Eastern Michigan University

Praise for Death Never Dies

Gold Medal in Pop Culture, IPPY Awards
Silver Medal in Anthologies, Midwest Book Awards

"Despite the strange title, this is actually a compelling anthology of writings from a number of gifted authors, the majority without significant name recognition. The same can be said for the essay subjects. While you will find a tribute to Ruth Bader Ginsberg and Breonna Taylor, you will also find more than one name here that you do not recognize and wonder how you missed their lives. The various viewpoints provided thought provoking questions about the effect of their lives on society. This book is about legacy." Midwest Book Awards

Also by Lee Fearnside

Friends of Friends of Friends: Defining and Building Community

Death Never Dies:
Mourning 2020 through the Lives and Deaths of Public Figures

The Field Guide to Animal Adaptations

O! Relentless Death: Celebrities, Loss, and a Year of Mourning
(with Andrew Fearnside)

Spark: Celebrities, Representation and Decisive Moments

Edited and Illustrated by
Lee Fearnside

with essays by

Roshelle Amundson	Hakim Bellamy
Erin Boyle	Coe Colette
Hermione Flavia	Ashley Geiger
Laureli Ivanoff	Roxane Llanque
John Mauk	D.S. Mohan
Michelle Otero	Lyndee Phillips
Rachel Richardson	Sandra Rivers-Gill
Emma Snyder	Robin Stock
D.J. Whisenant	Jennie Young

CHIMERA PROJECTS

Toledo, Ohio
2024

A Chimera Projects LLC Publication
www.ChimeraProjects.art

First Edition, October 2024

ISBN 978-1-7320964-7-9

© 2024 Lee Fearnside
© 2024 illustrations by Lee Fearnside
Cover Design by VM Design © 2024

Each essay © 2024 its author: Roshelle Amundson, Hakim Bellamy, Erin Boyle, Coe Colette, Hermione Stroud, Ashley Geiger, Laureli Ivanoff, Roxane Llanque, John Mauk, D.S. Mohan, Michelle Otero, Lyndee Phillips, Rachel Richardson, Sandra Rivers-Gill, Emma Snyder, Robin Stock, D.J. Whisenant, Jennie Young

No parts of this publication may be reproduced, stored in a retrieval system, or transmitted in any form or by any means, electronic, mechanical, photocopying, recording, or otherwise, without the prior written permission of the copyright owner.

Acknowledgments

This book wouldn't happen without the help of many. I thank the Smithie Long-Distance Bad A** Book Club, as you've seen me through all my celebrity crushes (and so much more) during the last three decades. Special thanks to my beta reader, Diana Wagner. Rachel Richardson convinced me to tackle another anthology during a chance encounter in the Kroger dairy aisle. Catherine Harrington helped with her indomitable copyediting. This project and Chimera Projects is supported in part by American Rescue Plan Act (ARPA) funds allocated by the City of Toledo and the Lucas County Commissioners and administered by The Arts Commission. As with all my projects, many thanks to my family, without whom none of this would happen.

Contents

Introduction

1 — We're All Christina Applegate
Jennie Young

7 — David
Laureli Ivanoff

14 — Behind the Speakers with Joan Jett
John Mauk

21 — The Complicated Business of Loving Joe Burrow
Robin Stock

33 — Panhandling for Peace: Resilience in the Fight for Joy
Roshelle Amundson

41 — Home for World-Weary Hearts
Erin Boyle

49 — The Letter I Never Wrote
Sandra Rivers-Gill

57 — Spill Into Everything, No Longer Ignoring Grief
Coe Collette

65 — Marilyn Monroe Dies; Pills Blamed
Emma Snyder

70 — Girls like Girls: the Revolutionary Reverie of Hayley Kiyoko
Roxane Llanque

77 — Can Yaman
D.S. Mohan

83 — Music Saves Lives.
D.J. Whisenant

87 — Shirley Temple
Hermione Flavia

95 — My Celebrity: Mary Ann Csipkay-Stadler
Lyndee Phillips

99 — Love Don't Hate (It Might Make America Great): A Journey with James Baldwin
Ashley Geiger

105 — Ani
Rachel Richardson

115 — A Eulogy for Dr. Heathclifford Huxtable…from a Cosby Kid
Hakim Bellamy

121 — In Search of Mexicans in Hollywood
Michelle Otero

127 — Contributor Biographies

Introduction

Celebrities, public figures and pop culture phenomena inspire us to understand our identities, our decisions and pivotal moments in our lives. Some are household names and megastars; some are relatively unknown but have a small group of loyal followers. While we may never really know celebrities, we may feel connected to them based on who or what they represent and how that reflects moments in our own lives. Celebrities may be heroes, villains, signposts or temporary influences. They may be our crushes, our deities, or people we love to mock. Chance encounters can make us feel vicariously famous. These essays explore how our connections can spark insight and investigation.

I was inspired to create this anthology by the death of Sinéad O'Connor. When I heard of her passing, I was transported back to my childhood bedroom and my teen years. I remember listening to the Lion and the Cobra when I was 14, maybe a year after its release. I was a freshman in high school, lonely, confused and filled with angst. I lay on my bed, staring at the light reflected from the spinning vinyl album on the ceiling. I remember feeling like her voice was in my blood, surging through my veins like an infection. After she died, I realized we were only eight years apart in age. She was only 21 when Lion and the Cobra was released, only 26 when she ripped up the Pope's photograph on Saturday Night Live. Now that I'm 50, it all feels impossibly young. Sinéad was *young* when she died. Her impact on my teen self at particularly vulnerable moments makes me feel like I somehow knew her, that the sound of her voice as those thoughts rolled through my mind was actually a conversation, even though I know (and knew) that was an illusion.

We all need things bigger than ourselves to make sense of the world. Sometimes those things are people, and rightly or wrongly, they help us understand something about ourselves.

Lee Fearnside
October, 2024

"We're All Christina Applegate"

I'm the same age as Christina Applegate. I'm also the same age that her breakout character, Kelly Bundy, the dumb blonde daughter of Al and Peggy Bundy on Married with Children, would be now. My fascination with Christina Applegate started back in those years. From 1987 until 1997, I watched the show primarily for her, and the reason I was so captivated is that even as a teenager, I understood that in order to play someone that dumb, Christina Applegate had to be really, really smart. And to go to another level of nuance, I suspected, and I think a lot of girls suspected, that beneath Kelly Bundy's hair-flips, mispronounced words, and "slutty" outfits, even within her fictional character there resided a specific kind of genius. We also knew that being blonde and promiscuous had no relationship to intelligence, other than that you maybe needed more intelligence to survive being blonde and promiscuous.

In the late 80's and early 90's, just being a pretty girl rendered you presumptively dumb. We were all accused of being dumb all the time, on a spectrum of "typical woman dumb" to "blonde woman dumb," the degree of dumbness correlating directly to the lightness of one's hair. And since blonde hair was the preferred hair color for pretty women in those days, the more insidious implication is that dumbness was also directly correlated with attractiveness.

So, girls were all dumb in those days, at least as a baseline quality. We were "airheads" and "ditzes" and "space cadettes," and those were the cute and funny names. It seems strange to me now that we so easily accepted our role as the punchline, the foil to smart and logical men. Every now and then some female character would be revealed as brainy, and this was always a surprise, an anomaly. If she were also pretty, it was as though a unicorn had been discovered, and nobody ever seemed to have any problem with fetishizing the "pretty girl who, OH MY GOD, is also smart!!!"

Between Kelly Bundy and Jen Harding in the deliciously dark and vicious comedy Dead to Me, I mostly lost track of Christina Applegate, focused as I was on my own life and career. But from the first episode of Dead to Me, I was transfixed. Christina Applegate was all grown up, and she was just like me and my friends. She was such a bitch, and we LOVED her. The series pulls no punches and spares no one; it conveys an allegiance to the brutal reality of stone-cold, "Capital T" truth, and it never makes that truth pretty.

But Applegate never chose pretty over truth. When she was diagnosed with breast cancer at the age of 36, she made the quite-literally "radical" decision to have a double mastectomy. Though her doctors suggested a course of radiation and continued monitoring, Applegate decided she was "just going to let them go,"[1] Hollywood beauty standards be damned. She did a nude photo shoot right before her surgery, even as she thought, "My God, I'm going to be butchered, and it's going to be horrible." And then she went directly under the knife.

That's a level of bad-assery difficult to comprehend, and yet it was only the beginning. According to the New York Times, in 2018, while filming a dance scene in the first season of Dead to Me, she "found herself off balance. Later, her tennis game began to falter. At the time, Applegate, an actress with an aversion to special pleading, didn't make excuses. She had to work harder, she told herself. She had to try again."

She worked harder and tried again for three more years, before finally being diagnosed with multiple sclerosis while still filming the third and final season in 2021. "I wish I had paid attention," she said. "But who was I to know?" Looking back, she realized she'd been having symptoms for years.

Why didn't she go to the doctor before it got so bad?! people wondered. And American women collectively threw back our heads and laughed.

Here's why she didn't go to the doctor: Because she was fucking busy. And because she probably knew the doctor would most likely just pat her on the head and offer a prescription for antidepressants, the proverbial bone-toss to all women who have the gall to show up at the doctor's while not actively giving birth, having a heart attack, or bleeding out.

I was once sent home from three different emergency rooms with diagnoses from "overactive bladder" to "cramps," before the fourth emergency room finally ran a CT scan and discovered a life-threatening blood clot in my abdomen that had been there all along. The doctor told me to immediately sit in this wheelchair and not to move because of the internal bleeding, that I would be promptly admitted and taken into surgery—I wasn't even allowed to go home and get my stuff. He also shook his head and said, "Honestly, I don't really understand how you're even up and walking around. Usually when people have something like this they complain a lot more, they seem way worse."

Was this my fault? Where, I wondered, was the sweet spot on the complaining spectrum that would secure medical care while not seeming hysterical? I stared at him blankly while laughing at him inside my head. That very morning I'd gone to the grocery store, unloaded and carried in all the groceries, and gone on a 5-mile run during which I stopped each mile to curl over in pain and re-gather my breath before soldiering on. I mean, I just "had cramps." I didn't want to be a baby.

Women have always been socialized to suffer.

But to suffer quietly, and to keep working, of course. To keep having babies, to keep taking care of the babies, to keep cooking, to keep tending to everyone else, to keep filming the third and final season of their blockbuster Netflix series, which is exactly what Applegate did.

She was urged by producers and other "powers that be" to simply stop, to throw something together to end the series, but after a five-month pause during which she began treatment for MS, Applegate said "No. We're going to do it, but we're going to do it on my terms."

And then she did something that was arguably even braver than continuing to work in the face of a crushing illness: she went on camera 40 pounds heavier than she'd been just the season before. She often couldn't walk without a cane. She entertained no illusions about the potential fallout of any of this, stating, "If people hate it, if people love it, if all they can concentrate on is, 'Ooh, look at the cripple,' that's not up to me. . . . I'm sure that people are going to be, like, 'I can't get past it.'" Applegate's response to that hypothetical: "Fine, don't get past it, then." She also acknowledged that she's constantly "pissed" and that she deals with the whole thing by watching reality TV in bed as a form of meditation.

This is why we Gen X women love her. She's just like us. The Millennials can have their Instagram wellness accounts and their self-care and their mental-health days and their commitment to yoga and meditation; we Gen X-ers were latchkey kids, and we prefer to survive our hardships by bitching and watching TV in bed.

Applegate totally killed it in Season Three. She was even better than in the first two seasons. There's a rawness and an edge to her performance in the final season that doesn't seem as though it could have been achieved out of thin air, though if anyone could pull it off maybe Christina Applegate could have. I think the more likely explanation is what we're all learning the older we get: for all of us, life inevitably gets hard, and shitty, and ugly, and just stupid. And it's the hardness and shittiness and ugliness and stupidity that makes us better, or at least that makes us funnier, and Christina Applegate is wickedly funny; she always has been.

We feel seen in the bitter darkness of Dead to Me's brand of humor; we get it. I was recently at the funeral of the husband of one of my best friends. It was "complicated," because they were separated and in the process of divorce when he died completely unexpectedly at the age of 51, literally dropped dead on the back porch. There was a group of six of us "girls" who'd been friends since grade school, the last of the funeral gang, sitting at one big, round table that we'd claimed as our own in the basement of the church, same as we used to in our high school cafeteria. We were the tragic nexus of a whirl of post-service activity in which church ladies busily cleared tables and wrapped up leftovers to send home with the new widow, who was a vegan food-snob and would never eat them anyway. Her two teenagers, still in shock, were around somewhere, cocooned in their own groups of friends from school and their cross-country team.

Everyone in that church basement except the six of us was crying. I don't know why we weren't crying. We HAD cried, of course, but now we just kept looking at each other saying, "Well, what the fuck?" For some reason I chose that moment to share my revelation that, from this point forward, when faced with one of those questionnaires that requires women to choose "single, married, divorced, separated, or widowed," my friend could reasonably write in "all of the above."

To say this cracked up the whole table would be an understatement. We absolutely roared. It was awkward for everyone around us, but we didn't care. I feel like Christina would have laughed with us.

The new widow had had her own breast cancer scare a few years earlier. It fortunately turned out better than Applegate's, but during the interim period of waiting, my friend just kept going to work and doing everything, same as Applegate did. During the time between mammogram and results that Applegate described as an "excruciating waiting period," my friend appeared to be totally fine. I challenged her on this, certain she was hiding her true feelings, but by way of explanation she shot back, "Look, I either don't have breast cancer, which would be awesome, or I do, which means everyone'll have to be nice to me. Either way, I win."

It's this specific outlook and attitude that's difficult to explain but that I sense Christina Applegate would totally get. She just keeps going. She doesn't pretend things are better than they are, nor does she dramatize them into anything worse. In the immediate aftermath of her diagnosis, "There was the sense of, 'Well, let's get her some medicine so she can get better,' . . . And there is no better." She added that she's not going to "come out on the other side of it, like, 'Woohoo, I'm totally fine,' . . . No. I'm never going to accept this."

I think this is what fighting spirit looks like when the fighting is no longer cute, when it's no longer "scrappy" or marketable or glittering with rom-com optics. This is fighting spirit in its grittier and more reality-based form. It's not a colorful character trait so much as a manifestation of human survival, and it's Christina Applegate's basic and humble humanity at this point in her life, which has been big and bright and faceted by complexity, which now surfaces with the shine of truth.

I wish she could go out to lunch with my girlfriends and me and we could all sit around and drink coffee and discuss what a beautiful shitshow life becomes at middle age. Amidst so much that feels phony—the curated collective of contemporary life—Christina Applegate feels real, and there's an irony in that. She's a lifelong actress; her whole life has hinged on successfully portraying other characters. We're just now finding out that the most fascinating character, not to mention the funniest and strongest character, was just her all along.

David

On my way home from to Unalakleet, a tiny fishing and hunting community on the west coast of Alaska, the Keflavik airport was the second of five stops. From the duty-free shop, I was happy to score two bags of Tritlar, a chocolate covered black licorice, along with a black wool sweater for my four-year-old son. At the gate I sat down next to a passenger with a small, shorthaired brown dog. Not wanting to be cooped up in a capsule with 100 other people for longer than necessary, I typically wait at the gate to be one of the last to board the flight.

As the gate emptied, I got in line and realized my patience in boarding worked in my favor. Looking outside the window to the tarmac I noticed passengers for Flight 681 to Seattle were being bussed from the gate to our aircraft. I'd, no doubt, be getting in the last bus and the jet's wheels would sooner or later pull up from the isle of Iceland.

Thirty other people waited in line, all of us filed neatly between the ribbon stanchions erected for order and movement. An elderly white couple stood in line behind me. I enjoyed the way the couple spoke to one another.

"That woman wasn't very helpful was she?" the wife said of the gate agent checking our passports and marking our tickets with a lilac marker before we entered the line. Her husband gave a quiet, air blowing through the nose giggle. "But she had nice fingernails," the white-haired woman said, her tone loaded with the twisted compliment. That's when I smiled and looked behind me, so the woman knew I got a kick out of her attitude.

Looking back at the couple, I saw him.

Then I immediately turned around to message my husband, back at home. "Fucking Dave Matthews is on my flight."

"!!!! What?!!" Timm messaged.

"Yeah," I said. I had not paid extra for international cell service, so Timm and I were messaging on Instagram. "He's in the economy line. [laughing tears emoji]"

Here's the thing. I'm not easily excited when seeing celebrities of any sort. As a journalist I've talked to people with influence and prestige. Also, I live in Alaska. Rural Alaska, where being pragmatic is of the highest value. In my mind, movie stars, unless they're cool, aren't very interesting. Politicians, unless they're cool, only say what's scripted. Sports stars, unless they're cool, operate from ego. Musicians, unless they write their own lyrics, play multiple instruments, are up-to-date on social issues and use their voice to speak out against oppression, and are standing right there, affably talking with a mother, daughter, and teenage granddaughter trio who have no idea who they're talking with, are self-absorbed.

"I'm kind of self-absorbed," I hear him jokingly say to the women.

Knowing I could get another look without showing on my face I was completely starstruck, I turn around. He's wearing black leather shoes, black jeans, a black t-shirt, a black canvas-type jacket with a dark gray scarf. He was with a woman, not his wife, maybe an assistant. Then Fucking Dave Matthews looks right at me and I feel our eyes lock. Playing it cool, I turned the corner of my lips just slightly, put some warmth to my eyes, and gave the teeniest hint of a nod before turning back around.

In. Absolute. Awe.

This sounds overblown, but it isn't. It was like the awe when standing on ocean ice and hearing the breathing of a white whale before seeing it. Scanning the water to see the slippery looking pale skin under the blue water, waiting to see it surface. Once it does, hearing the pop of the air moving out and upward, followed by air moving through a tube in, oxygen filling the beluga's lungs. Rare. Beautiful. Wild.

This is really happening.

I need to get a photo with him, I thought. How do I do that without being creepy?

Once in the bus and now actually rubbing elbows, with my back straight, my head held high, I ask him, "Can I get a photo?"

"Yes," he kindly said as we moved further into the bus so the remaining passengers could file through.

We stood close to one another, and I took the selfie.

I figured that would be that and he'd go back to talking with the woman he was traveling with.

"I feel like I know you," he said. Or maybe he said. "I feel like we've met before." Or maybe he said. "Have we ever met?" But he did say, "I feel like we have and it's kind of messing with me." Or maybe he said, "and it's kind of freaking me out."

"No. We've never met." I said, "I'm from a little fishing and hunting town in northwest Alaska."

Realizing we were going to chat, I felt my face get hot. It was probably a bit flushed. I felt my heart beat in my chest. My underarms got sweaty.

Damn, I'm not playing it cool.

I asked why he was in Reykjavik. He said he was in Amsterdam visiting his son who's going to school there. That he and his sister decided to spend some time on the way back to the US in Iceland. They drove around the island and enjoyed their visit.

"I spent Christmas here a number of years ago," I said. To Dave Matthews. He had great eye contact. While telling him how people on island countries have a strong identity, I realized his eyes reminded me of the apple caramel lollipops that hit grocery store shelves before Halloween.

He asked why I was in Iceland. I told him I am a writer and that I was in Finland. I told him I was contributing to a book by Indigenous writers throughout the circumpolar north and that visual artists would create pieces in response to our writings.

"Do you have a publication date?" he asked.

Or maybe he asked, "When are you publishing?"

But I said, "We have a publisher. We don't have a timeline yet."

He seemed genuinely interested in the idea of Indigenous visual artists responding to Indigenous writers' work. He seemed like he genuinely wanted to see the book.

I then told him it was really nice to be around other artists and writers who are like minded and who have a similar history of…

"Similar history of oppression," he said.

"Yes, exactly," I said. "It was really affirming and encouraging, spending time with all of them. Writing truth can be difficult sometimes."

We continued talking throughout the bus ride. We didn't really stop talking until we were climbing the stairs to the plane. At one point I told him about the little town I live in. How we live simply. How we love it. How we live in direct relationship with the land and water. How this relationship of respect is a critical component missing in the dominant western society. We talked about the unsustainability of capitalistic culture.

"But how much can one person do?" I said. To Dave Matthews.

Dave mentioned something he read. A study done on mice. When the population exploded, it was the mice that quietly and peacefully went about getting food that survived. The high-strung mice all died out. He said something about how it's going to be communities like mine that will likely survive a major event.

I agreed and he grabbed his phone and asked how to spell my hometown. He wanted to read about it while on the flight. I asked to take his phone. He handed it over. I typed in Unalakleet, Alaska. I wanted to google my name so he could read my writings about Unalakleet, but I felt shy. I didn't want to be too forward. But I should have been. I'm not that cool, I thought.

Nearing the top of the stairs, before I found my seat in economy, him in First Class, he asked, "What's your name?"

"I'm Laureli. Ivanoff."

"Laureli Ivanoff," he repeated. "That's a great name."

I nodded with a slight smile, in agreement.

He then held out his hand.

"I'm David," he said.

"David," I said, with a quiet, air-blowing-through-the-nose laugh. "Nice to meet you."

"Nice to meet you, Laureli Ivanoff," he said.

The flight from Reykjavik to Seattle was nearly eight hours. With the bussing of the passengers, we left more than an hour late. Once landing and with a tight connection, I quickly made my way to the plane's exit, knowing I likely wouldn't get to again see the artist I had just met.

But after securing my bag from the baggage claim, making my way toward Passport Control, there he stood, waiting for his luggage.

"It was really nice meeting you, David," I said in passing.

"It was really mice meeting you, Laureli, cheers." he said. Or maybe it was, "Nice meeting you, Laureli, cheers" Or maybe it was, "Thanks, nice meeting you, Laureli, cheers," but either way, Fucking Dave Matthews knew my name.

Before our plane left Iceland soil, I posted the photo on Instagram and Facebook. I thought I should be cool and wait, but I couldn't. In the caption I wrote, "Just had a good 20-minute visit with a new friend named David (how he introduced himself).

We chatted about the progressiveness of the Indigenous mindsets, the book I was in Finland discussing, and Unalakleet."

A day later I was home and my body and mind still buzzed from the encounter. I played songs by Dave Matthews Band on repeat from my iPhone, as I did on the remaining three flights it took to land in Unalakleet. I boisterously told my friends and anyone who asked about meeting with and talking with David Matthews, recounting the eye contact and his understanding of Indigenous challenges. My husband, after the third day, was worn from my stories about the artist.

"Just one more thing and then I'll be quiet about Dave Matthews," I told Timm. "Remember he was flying with his sister?" I asked. "Listen to this song. He wrote it about her." I then made him listen to the song he wrote about his baby sister, Jane, the live version recorded at Radio City Music Hall with Tim Reynolds.

After hearing the lyrics, I let myself be quiet about my encounter with a celebrity I respect. I let myself relish in the moments we shared getting on a plane in Keflavik, Iceland. I listened to his tunes while home alone, writing or cleaning.

But ever since I've kicked myself for not typing in my website, laureliivanoff.com, so that David Matthews could read my writings about home. Because, I realized, I am only one person. Writing is what I do. And I'll use my voice to say we live in direct relationship with the land and water. I'll say the relationship of respect is a critical component missing in the dominant western society.

Laureli Ivanoff

Behind the Speakers with Joan Jett

In my youth, I played rock and roll, lots of it. At fourteen, I started a career path that traveled through countless bars, clubs, and theaters. From New York to Chicago, Detroit to Austin, premier venue to back-alley rathole, I can still recall the stages: chewed-up floorboards, sticky railings, mealy carpet, duct tape debris, and candy-colored lights shining down. I came to understand the gross semi-relief of dressing rooms: re-purposed janitorial closets with utility sinks, full basements deemed unworthy of public use, at least one attic, and a few band houses that prompted us to sleep fully clothed, in the truck, or at a hotel. It was a working-class life. We traveled hundreds of miles each week, performed three to five nights at a time, and regularly saw sunrise from the backside. I still live according to a bandmate's declaration, something he muttered as the dull glow of morning misted into the sky: it's not tomorrow until you sleep first.

In the late 80's, we often played The Power Company, a mid-sized club in central Ohio that attracted a cross-section of humans: fashion-forward twenty-somethings, middle-aged professionals, blue-collar workers. They poured themselves into a soupy mass of Dionysian gusto, and it was in that club—on some random night in '88 or '89—I realized something fundamental, something that rewires the machinery of awareness.

The clock was breaching midnight, that pivotal moment when ideology begins to forget itself and concepts start rubbing shoulders with their opposites—when yin and yang leap over coordinates and scare themselves a little. After a collective hoist of beverages and a beer-fueled yawp—the kind of crowd roar that curls you inward—I scanned all those whipped-up people draniing their bottles of beer or Zima and understood my job in the clearest light. It was the opposite of Saul falling from his horse, seeing a cross in the sky. I was not meant to conquer in any sign but to attract masses and keep them thirsty. I was in league with bartenders and beer taps, my musical efforts a catalyst for consumption, nothing more.

In that moment and for years thereafter, my revelation generated some self-loathing, disdain for live performance, even my own instruments. I resented being a tool, and beneath that resentment lay a tangle of flawed assumptions about rock music, performers, and identity.

I took a hiatus and tried academic life. After a few years of graduate English studies, the old ways beckoned. My senses missed the pressure of 90hz against my legs, the methodical politics of soundcheck, the squawk of stage monitors, even the yeasty funk of old beer that fuses to clothes and instrument cases. I heeded the call and returned to rock with an all-original band. It was the 90's. Seattle's influence had refashioned the zeitgeist. Mainstream rock looked different from years prior. It had a new snarl (perhaps a grimace), but frequencies worked as they always had. Sonic fundamentals persisted as did that old function: musicians were needed to keep the nightlife economy rolling.

My band garnered various contracts and all forms of institutional support. We went hard, making it out to CBGB, the New Music Café, and prog rock venues through the Midwest. From underground urban club to outdoor festival, studio to studio, we found ourselves deep inside the folds of rock culture. And when I remember those days, the weird collage of labor and artistic energy, I often return to a few semi-quiet moments with Joan Jett. It was an outdoor show in our hometown of Toledo. We made our way to the riverfront, wormed around the barricades, and inched our trailer into the loading zone. After rolling gear toward the stage, we got some news: we'd get a full sound check—hallelujah—not a huffy line test often designated for opening bands. (Before you're a known entity, event managers, stage crew, agents, sound techs, bouncers, and staffers of all stripes grant themselves license to demean you, but if you gain any traction in the industry's slip-sliding chaos, an occasional bit of grace falls from the sky, and on this summer, '95 or '96, we'd gained traction. Radio was turning friendly, big venues were taking our calls, and so on. Still, a full sound check with a major national act? Quite a gift.)

With a crowd gathering, we played through a couple songs. Our crew was dialing us in, early audience members watching the pre-show calculus. At one point, I looked to my left and saw a short, tough-looking woman with serious arms nodding to the beat. After getting a distant thumbs-up from our soundman, I pulled off my guitar and went behind the speakers—a slim corridor that follows the backside of PA cabinets. It's not backstage but stage-adjacent, an off- and on-ramp, an existential funnel, liminal space where bands break up, managers yell at roadies, drummers finally take a swing, aids deliver oxygen, and singers slug a bottle or vomit. It's not private, not where performers become their pre-iconic selves, nor is it public, where they must pitch their personas outward. It's operational, a transition zone, neither dressing nor press room. It's a pathway marked by transformation: you're either becoming or abandoning an ultra-public face. Anything may get uttered, but it's always pressurized by performance. The crowd, after all, is just beyond the great wall.

Until then, I'd only seen Joan Jett on television—her famous spikey hair, brazen eyeliner, and black leather—so I had to assure myself the tough-looking woman was her. She had none of her accoutrements but stood with a comfortable assurance. She spoke first. "Good songs," she said—with a smokey tone that comes only from years of heavy singing.

I don't remember my response but said something resonant enough to launch a conversation. Standing there with an audience fomenting, we got into songwriting. I asked about her early years—who, for instance, wrote "Waitin' for the Night?" Her answer began with, "Well, it's hard to say…" a polite threshold into a more serious exchange about collaboration, ensemble, and reception. Crew members were shooting back and forth, random staffers skirting around and leaving us in our rhetorical bubble. Given the season (full-on summer), the weather (hardcore sunny), and her status (rock star), she could've worn shades, but she didn't. This wasn't the onstage rocker who doesn't give a damn about her bad reputation, nor the well-managed ethos that would reinforce such disregard. It wasn't even the backstage handshaker who greets fans and signs autographs. This was the working musician, Joan Jett.

****

Literary critics bifurcate authors. They cleave the human-who-creates into two entities: the author and the implied author. They're different. For instance, the Toni Morrison who woke up with headaches or stomach woes or neither is not the Morrisonian voice in Beloved, Jazz, or The Song of Solomon. The person we all now speak of when we say Toni Morrison is an implied entity, one shaped by the genre, the craft, and countless utterances around textuality. In other words, the world of scholarship and readership determines who Toni Morrison is, has been, and will be. No matter how much biographical research we might undertake, we will not know—or get closer to knowing—the woman who woke up and wrote those beautiful novels. All that research will simply (or miraculously) add to the image we have of the novelist.

Lately, I'm inclined to join what literary people have separated. The working artist and the performed entity twist and writhe together. They travel in the same van but take the mic at different times. As the mighty Canadian rock band Rush declared, "All the world is, indeed, a stage and we are merely players." (Someone else, at some point, may have said something similar.) We all know this. Social media reinforces it daily. But the grand stage is multi-dimensional. There are offshoots, spatial tentacles where we get to play some other role, something divergent. We attenuate and tweak according to the moment.

Lately, I've been seeing the word authentic. Be your authentic self. Give people authentic experiences. The notion, apparently, has value to educators and marketers. Was Joan somehow more authentic with me? Not really. Or maybe. It doesn't matter. When you live a theatrical life—when you work hard to build an ethos meant for consumption—you don't put much stock in authenticity, real-ness, genuineness. Instead, you see your self, that buzzwordy notion borne of terrible philosophy and even worse politics, as a matter of function not essence. You work, help, struggle, join forces, abandon missions, conjure new goals, love, hate, destroy, rebuild, and rock onward until the end. Or maybe you rock onward after the end. I don't know. But I know this: along the way, you serve functions. You do what an industry, community, family, and culture want. You act accordingly or buck or both. And all those acts, all the faces you present, accrete into something you might eventually, on a deathbed or post-life cloud, call yourself. Or better yet, you stay quiet and let history conjure your essence.

So, did I meet the real Joan Jett? Absolutely. Not Joan Marie Larkin, the woman who wakes up and yells at her dog, cat, lover, hamster, or whomever, not the shrewd businesswoman who calculates the payoff of specific gigs, advertisements, and tours, not the Joan with dying friends or medical appointments of her own, not the Joan who hates (or loves) her neighbors, who hates (or loves) pasta, who votes or doesn't vote in ways counter to her fans' expectations. All those dimensions were absent in that space behind the speakers. But I met a quieter Joan than the rest of the world typically sees, a humble and reflective Joan who was willing to share insights with an upstart. In that veiled corridor, we were two working rock singers, not far afield from two plumbers discussing conduit types.

Here's another thing I know: rock performers sell booze, records, and bric-a-brac called merchandise, but they also usher us away from the proper dimensions of everyday life. They take us by the ears and yank us headlong into transgression—usually a mild form, an emotional and physical state from which we can easily return when the night is over, when the lights flicker on, when the sun comes back to sober up the sky. I don't believe I'm overstating rock's curative force—its stabilizing function within a tentative republic. People need the temporary release, the joy of profanity. Just as European serfs needed carnivals to invert power structures—to parody aristocrats, to behead royals—we quasi-modern Americans need rituals of transgression. We also need someone or something to lead us into carnivalesque rites. As any stage performer can attest, people are always ready, poised for drama, retaliation, even rapture. It only takes the right song, the right speech, the right megaphone. If rock or one of its sibling genres isn't the guide, it will be something more destructive, more seditious.

I no longer disdain my early years. I'm less cynical now, less offended. Time flushed away toxic beliefs, uncountable notions that make people imagine some inherent value beyond utility. In my youth, I was a tool, a living apparatus of the entertainment sector, a small element in a big economy. I'm good with it, all of it. Nietzsche was right. Essence is a nonsensical phantom, a fever-dream for romantics and other dangerous creatures.

****

As the 90's and its agonistic fashion sense gave way to a new century, I stepped away from stages and plunged back into academia. I traded noise for quiet. I learned how to thrive in non-rock existence and acquired the role of college professor and writer. It wasn't easy or smooth, but time and a penchant for introversion made it possible. I'm now old enough to see the broad strokes of a narrative: my formative years were dedicated to the economics of mild transgression, my latter to a self-aggrandizing parasitic aristocracy. I have been catalyst for both. How do I hope history tags me? Which do I prefer? The prior, no doubt. But I have little choice in the matter.

Before Joan took the stage, I saw her from a distance with her eyes outlined, legs wrapped in leather, and hair roostering upward. I ran around the great wall, the one that divides spectators from spectacle makers, and stood back fifty yards to watch she and her Blackhearts hammer the daylights out of their instruments. The short quiet woman from stage-adjacent was now controlling the din of thousands. She could say anything and provoke a roar. We must acknowledge this: the peril of celebrities. They mount their stages and call forward whatever reinforces their own standing, which often amounts to the worst discourses of an era—the daft and reactionary, the dismissive and coarse, the materialistic and petty—but some manage the poetics of transgression. They understand their own function. Their aesthetic follows the contours of abandonment, the impulse to escape quotidian life, not topple it. They give voice to freedom not destruction. Hail, thus, the working rocker. More importantly, hail the benign celebrity, the one who comprehends the slim pathways, who takes us on a brief rogue tour but gladly returns us to an un-wrecked civilization.

John Mauk

The Complicated Business of Loving Joe Burrow

It was fucking cold out.

That's what I remember most. The four of us huddled together under some weird picnic blanket, not one of us dressed appropriately for the weather. It might have been late November, or maybe early December. My kids were seven and eleven. The younger one was missing a tooth. He refused to wear a coat. The older one kept asking when we could leave.

I was a kind-of, sort-of, football fan then. I understood it a little. And I liked the excitement surrounding this particular game. The whole town of Athens seemed to be out, not nearly filling a whole section of the massive, iconic "Horseshoe" in Columbus. Our little group was loud and excitable, all wearing variations of the Athens High School green and gold, or something representing the green and white of Ohio University. The players had all colored their hair green and gold. This game, for Athens, was a Big Deal.

The Athens High School football team were massive underdogs in a state championship game against a sports powerhouse of a private school in Toledo. As the season had stretched on, Athens became more and more interested in its high school football program, powered by senior Joe Burrow. Something magical was happening with each win, and the whole town felt it.

So, on that day in early winter, the town showed up to watch Joe Burrow play his final high school game. Joe Burrow, son of one of the coaches at Ohio University. Joe Burrow, the Athens boy who had already committed to play at The Ohio State University. Joe Burrow, who was surely bound to make his hometown proud.

The game was a back-and-forth that some sports reporters later called a "battle of titans." Later, the Athens High School coach would say it was clear early in the game that it would simply come down to "whoever was left standing in the end." Despite the cold, there was no leaving early. The game came down to the very last seconds, with Athens losing 56 to 52.

There was no shame in the loss Athens suffered that night, not for anyone from Athens. Later, Joe would say it was the worst day of his young life. He threw an interception that he could not shake from his "what if" list. To this day, he references that game, the mistakes he thinks he made. But for the collective us? We were happy to be able to show up, to show the bigger schools that our little high school in the Hocking Hills could hang with the big dogs.

I have felt this way plenty since then, mostly related to my own son's growing aptitude for soccer. When his club team out of Logan, Ohio—population 7,332—beat expensive, arrogant club teams from Columbus in the MOSSL tournament back in 2019, I could not have been prouder. I had that same feeling. See, you arrogant fuckers? You don't have to pay thousands of dollars a year to pull together a winning team. I still feel that way sometimes, even though we have invested a solid five figures into club play since then. I retain an underdog's mentality, that feeling that tenacity and scrappiness will always outshine legacy.

Seeing Joe play his heart out with his high school team, knowing he was about to go on to a massive Big Ten program? That was enough. He didn't need to win, not for the city of Athens, Ohio.

But then, after he went to OSU, he didn't play. He didn't play in year one, or year two, or year three. And I can only speak for myself in saying that I pretty much forgot about Joe Burrow. He simply wasn't a part of our football conversations anymore.

And then he was.

Suddenly, and seemingly out of nowhere, Joe Burrow was all anyone could talk about.

He was down in Louisiana, doing a master's degree at LSU. And he was playing football. He was winning.

Joey B was back on the national stage—still baby-faced and vanilla—bringing LSU closer and closer to a coveted national title with each game he played. It was like the magical high school season in 2014 all over again. Athens, for its part, was paying attention. The green and white town turned gold and purple for a season, t-shirts and signs emblazoned with the New Orleans-ified "Burreaux."

So Joe Burrow, showing out at LSU after practically disappearing for four years before? That was a Cinderella story. Joe, who literally did not play during his undergrad years, a finalist for the Heisman trophy? Cinderella. And, holy shit, Joe winning the Heisman trophy? Put on your ball gowns, people.

On December 14, 2019, Joe Burrow accepted his award. He cried through the whole of his speech. He thanked a bunch of people, including his coach, his O-line, and his parents. All the people you might expect. But then? He said this:

"Coming from southeast Ohio it's a very impoverished area and the poverty rate is almost two times the national average. There's so many people there that don't have a lot and I'm up here for all those kids in Athens and Athens County that go home to not a lot of food on the table, hungry after school. You guys can be up here, too."

The speech was probably ten minutes long and this quote was maybe thirty seconds of it. Thirty seconds.

If Athens wasn't proud of him before? It certainly was then.

The collective of Athens, Ohio felt seen, then. Not in a J.D. Vance, Hillbilly Ellegy way that condescended and disparaged the region. No, instead, Joe's comment made southeast Ohio feel like a place where there was poverty, but also hope. There was distress, but also opportunity.

Joe shared later that he was just saying what was in his heart. Of all the moments, on one of the biggest stages and with a professional contract on the horizon, Joe Burrow thought of the kids in Athens County who did not have enough to eat.

There wasn't a dry eye among any Athenian that night, I assure you.

Within days, more than $500,000 poured in from all over the country to support food insecurity in Joe's hometown. I swear I refreshed my Facebook feed every hour, just to see that number grow. It was exhilarating to watch.

Now, I realize what a significant risk it is to put any single human being on a pedestal. The NFL, in particular, has an inconsistent history when it comes to how it reacts to player behavior. They give out the Walter Payton Man of the Year Award to nice, white boy Eli Manning (who I do think is probably a pretty okay dude, so no disrespect) in the same year that Colin Kaepernick's career ended, simply because he took a knee to quietly protest the deaths of unarmed Black people at the hands of police. The award honors players who have done great work in philanthropy and community impact. To this day, the NFL has never honored Colin Kaepernick, who has had—arguably—some of the biggest impact on social justice of any player before him.

Celebrity offers a heavy mantle to wear, I would imagine. If a person fucks up, it can mean the end of a career, or it can mean the spotlight burns more brightly. Many NFL players are young, just out of college or having left college early for professional play. They are making a minimum of seven figures in most cases, more money than most of them could ever have dreamed of seeing, just to play a game in which they are encouraged to be violent.

Andrew Whitworth (who retired from the LA Chargers after their 2022 Superbowl win over the Cincinnati Bengals and—you guessed it—a second-year Bengals quarterback named Joe Burrow) called it a "child's game" when he accepted his own Walter Payton Man of the Year Award in 2022, and it is. Still, football is a game that puts grown men's bodies at risk with each play. ACLs get torn, legs get broken, and sometimes much worse. The NFL has been notoriously un-serious about concussion protocol for a long time. Former players were committing unspeakable acts of violence against themselves and others simply because they sustained too many head injuries playing this "child's game." Earlier this year, young Damar Hamlin took a blow to the chest that sent him into cardiac arrest. More than twenty years ago, a player for the Detroit Lions suffered a paralyzing spinal cord injury on the field. The game is violent. It is not for children.

At forty-seven—my age as of today—twenty-six-year-old Joe Burrow could be my child. I have never met the guy, despite the very small degree of separation we share (my mother-in-law was his school nurse and my father-in-law taught him at Athens High School). Still, I feel a great deal of pride for the man, for what he's done and accomplished—a feeling nearly akin to how I might feel should my own children reach the heights he has—in sports or otherwise. It feels moderately safe to say that Joe feels like "Athens' son," the joyfully collective creation of a town that is mostly known for being a party school or for being a step away from any other Hillbilly Elegy, Dopesick type of town. Seeing Joe thrive, seeing him succeed, seeing him get up and try again, those things bring great pride to all Athenians, I believe. You can walk uptown Athens and find shirts with his name and number, shirts that read "Just a Kid from Southeast Ohio" across the front.

Joe Burrow continues to make Athens proud. When he took the call to come play for the Bengals from his parents' house, he wore 740 on his shirt, representing the area code for Athens. When he signed the paperwork making him the highest played NFL player in history, he wore his Athens High School Football t-shirt. Those were deliberate choices, choices meant to articulate that he had not forgotten where he came from. Joe's actions are always thoughtful and measured, repeatedly proven.

On August 7, 2020, in response to another unarmed black man dead at the hands of police, Joe Burrow used his social media to tweet, "How can you hear the pain Black people are going through and dismiss it as nothing. How can you hear the pain and respond with anything other than, 'I stand with you.'"

On June 24, 2022, the U.S. Supreme Court overturned Roe V. Wade. Three days later, Joe Burrow used his Instagram page to make a statement about women's rights. These were meaningful statements, because the NFL fan base, while diverse, has a history of disinterest in hearing any kind of political commentary out of men whom they view as commodities.

It is not lost on me that there was no significant blowback on Joe Burrow for making those statements. He is a white man, a status that comes with a different kind of privilege than, say, the aforementioned Colin Kaepernick. The latter has become a volatile icon of civil rights. What happened to his career is nearly criminal, in my opinion, but his worth and impact as an activist, at this point, is likely more than his worth and impact as a football player.

But I digress again. The point, here, is that Joe Burrow seems to have been able to sneak under the wire with comments that might cause fury among the white, male, die-hard, beer-drinking football set. Except—they didn't. There may have been a few comments on social media, but Joe's brand suffered no damage. None. That same year, he founded the Joe Burrow Foundation to "provide resources and support to the underprivileged and underserved."

My point, in all of this, is twofold. One: I think Joe has been able to show character through the simplicity of his words and the quality of his actions. Two: I think he is earning that pedestal, but I have not forgotten that his ability to do so is a result of no small amount of privilege.

I went to my first Cincinnati Bengals game in December. As you might imagine, I was pretty damned excited. In the nine years since high school Joe played in that high school championship game, I have become a "real" football fan. Like, the kind that knows players names and positions, that knows what kind of problems might happen if two starters on the O-line's right side go out with injuries at the same time. I am now the kind of fan with a sticker on my car and a jersey in my closet.

It is so weird, but it happened. Pre-2020, I liked watching football but considered myself an agnostic about the teams. I never fully committed to being a team's "fan." Then, "The Bungles" drafted Joey B.

During his first season, the Cincinnati Bengals kind of retained that nickname. I watched, but then Joe got injured with an ACL tear that took him out for most of the season. The Bengals did a whole bunch of nothing. Most people don't even count that as a season for Joe. In 2021, though, he was back, so back, in fact, that he led the team to the Superbowl for the first time since 1989. The 2021 season cemented my support for the team—as it did for the whole of Cincinnati. The city was beside itself in love with their franchise quarterback.

When we went to the game this past year, I could barely contain myself. There was Joe, tossing the ball in warmups. Evan McPherson, who saved the team's collective ass with a magical kicking leg the season before, stood fifty feet away from where we sat. Jamar Chase was there to make explosive runs and catches. I was so down for all of it, but then the game started out as a game of punts, which

is boring to watch. No one was scoring.

The crowd around us was a mix of Cleveland Browns fans and Cincinnati Bengals fans. Most were cordial and friendly. Except for that one guy. There's always that one guy, right? The guy who comments "God, I hope that guy doesn't catch the ball again" after the on-field announcer botched the name Owusu-Koramoah. When embattled Deshaun Watson, the Cleveland quarterback, narrowly avoided a sack, the same guy said, "Bates is saying, 'I almost raped you'." At that point, I turned back and said, "Rape? Really?" He switched to calling Cleveland fans "Monkeybutt" after that, because I'm certain I looked like I might launch myself up and over two rows of seats had he made one more racist or sexist comment.

Sports is a complicated business. It brings out the best and worst in players and fans alike. I cannot say I haven't lost my temper on a ref at the soccer pitch. I can say with complete certainty that I have never used a racist or sexist slur during my temper tantrums, though. I may have screamed a little. (Okay, a lot.) But look, sport also has the power to connect people who are vastly different around a common goal: Win. It has the power to make strangers hug each other after a score. It has the power to make us hold our collective breath with real worry when a young kid goes down unresponsive after a hard hit.

In sport, stadiums of people who come from different races, cultures, and backgrounds rally around that singular, focused love of sport together. There are laborers and executives, fundraisers and auto mechanics, Black and white and brown, women and men and non-binary. All of them, for those three hours of a game, are together, united in the joy of watching elite athleticism.

This is not unique to football. Overseas, football is soccer, where the fans sing and bang on drums and chant. But there, too, they spew racist bullshit at elite players. English fans vilified Bukayo Saka, who missed a critical penalty shot at the Euro 2020 final, in such a significant way that he nearly didn't continue his career. Today, he plays many minutes for Arsenal, a Premier League team that is, arguably, one of the best in the league. Time Magazine named him one of their Next Generation Leaders in 2022, his story inspiring many young athletes. Even in high school sports, casual racism, sexism and homophobia are exhibited regularly.

These types of abuses make an argument that elite players are merely commodities to the fans. Players are not human, because they belong to the fans. And look, fans pay exorbitant ticket prices to watch live games. They spend money on expensive merchandise and they drink overpriced beer and eat overpriced food in the stadiums. All of this makes the teams, the league, and the players a shit-ton of money, and gives fans a sense of ownership that often slips into dangerous territory. If no one showed up to watch the Cincinnati Bengals, then how would the team be able to afford what is now the biggest quarterback contract in history? And since Joe has accepted this massive contract, will his performance match the amount of faith these dollars represent? In a fan's mind—right or wrong—that player is on the field to entertain. To perform. To win. For the fans.

Joe Burrow gave an interview after the Damar Hamlin incident, which happened in Cincinnati. He cared first about the well-being of both teams, and the well-being of Damar himself. He spoke of a "brotherhood" among players. But he also said that players understand that the game is dangerous, that they understand the risks that they take when they step on the field. I thought this was an interesting perspective, one that is playing out a bit this season already. Joe missed much of training camp due to a soft tissue injury and the Bengals started their season 0-2, with Joe leaving the first game in the fourth quarter, limping to the sideline, and showing visible frustration. He came back out in game three after being listed as "questionable," and if I had to guess, he felt the weight of that contract propelling him to lead his team regardless of his injury or level of pain. (The Bengals did get a critical win that game, by the way.)

I love sports. I love sitting on the sideline at my son's games, watching him put all of himself into something he loves. I love seeing his athleticism emerge and develop. When he blew his ACL at fourteen-years-old, he worried he wouldn't come back as the same player he was before the injury. I watched him work and push so that he could return to the field that fall, with some serious warning from his doctor, only to find his playing time limited, his team placement below his expectations, and his performance tentative. Now, eighteen months later, he plays many minutes in each game and I almost don't worry about his knee anymore. He knows there is risk in returning to sport, but he cannot imagine living without it and, as such, I can't either.

Christ, this shit is complicated. Loving a game, loving a team, loving a player—it is complicated. At least for me it is, because I care about people. I try to be a good role model. I try to speak out when I need to, for those who cannot speak for themselves, against injustice or abuse. I will absolutely put myself at risk to help someone else. So how does that jive when juxtaposed to loving a team or an athlete or a celebrity who ends up not being a very good human? As a rational person, all of this complexity can make it feel like a betrayal to love the game. If I love football, or soccer, am I betraying women? Am I betraying the Black community? Am I ignoring unethical behavior? Am I ignoring criminal behavior?

That feels gross to me. Players who beat their spouses and partners receive forgiveness if they help their teams win. Coaches who rain harmful emotional abuse on their players see their behaviors ignored if they win games. Doctors who abuse athletes behind closed doors are protected because they are keeping winners on the mats, on the hardwood, on the turf. We revere sports. We elevate it to kinghood and hold it above all else, including basic humanity.

My son and I talk a lot about being a good person, about being a good sport, about not being a shitty human, on and off the field. Our family has done service together in the community since our kids were small. We started conversations about consent when he was barely double digits. We talk about standing up for what is right. I would not put my son on a pedestal because he is human and, thus, fallible. He will screw up. He won't always get it right.

Neither will Joe Burrow. He is also a human, and he will falter at times. But after seeing him speak out for hungry kids, and women, and the Black community, I believe and hope that he will grow into a true leader for the football community, that he will continue to make Athens proud.

And I will be there, in my #9 jersey, every step of the way.

Robin Stock

Panhandling for Peace: Resilience in the Fight for Joy

I spent the evening rubbing essential oils into the weathered grooves of someone else's husband. Father. Grandfather. Prior to this bottle-based plant-healing, I lay on my side on the tile of their bathroom, gathered him to my chest—initially oblivious of the floor betraying his leaked-puddles dampening my clothes—and hugged and lifted him to sitting position while we awaited the paramedics. Why are we sitting on the floor? Jack blinked and widened his October-skies eyes with concussed confusion, slowly surrendering that mischievous smile despite the pain.

Jack and Jan live in the apartment down the hall from my mother; they have become our family. He's been more prone to weakness and falling recently; he is of failing health, and while no one has spoken it, we all understand the time draws closer. Not another one. The drift of grief in its crest has me riding that damn tide—again—not new to me. Him, him, her—lover, father, sister. Nine years ago, an onslaught of rapid take-aways of some of my most-loved in the span of twenty months. I survived it. That surprised me.

Jan had brought out a picture of him earlier in the day. Black-and-white era; Navy cap tilted to the side. "This is my baby," she lamented, gazing at the man she fell in love with over 60 years ago. Once again, she'll head to the hospital where she hopes he will remember her. He won't. "He's just gone downhill so fast," she cried, and there it is—the first time I've felt the weight of the slow-leaking loss of him to dementia, in her words. Not of the nights he's sunsetting, looking for the cigarettes he no longer smokes, adult diaper in hand, standing only in what God gave him in front of the patio doors of the senior-living complex—but the vanishing sailor she fell in love with.

Even the dog is depressed. He slumps in the chair of his master, too worn to lift his head, though he'll eat a treat for five-second consolation—a distraction from the empty chair, the empty room, the empty everything. There is nothing I can say to help him understand; that almost hurts me the most. Almost.

Meanwhile in a hospital bed across Lake Michigan lies my aunt. I am grateful that my mother misunderstood, and my beloved Carol is not in fact, at a rehab facility called the "Motor Lodge." What sort of Yooper-below-the-bridge-Billy-grab-your-crossbow would that have been? It's bow-hunting season, but before we scout for deer, let's stop and give patient M2435 hyper radiation in her metastasis. Ugly, sinister word.

The cancer began in the lungs and with the systemic delays in treatment, biopsy, CT and PET scans, the toxins sought more real estate in her brain. Because that's what lung cancer does. It is a permanent resident of those parentheses-shaped breathers, but it builds a summer home in the brain. And if we're going to talk

about the brain, let's really talk about that complicated cabbage at the top floor.

The complexity of post-pandemic times is an iron-burden we all drag behind us; in so, we are very much in for long-COVID recovery. The mirroring of sickened cell and tissue damage is our very humanity; every detail of our existence, from the grand to pithy—is now politicized under a binary microscope. The consequence? The data suggests that one in three Americans now suffers at least one form of mental-health issue. That is no less than an endemic.

When conducting a search on mental health, there are 3.42 billion results. The data appears (because Google thought I should know) in 0.68 seconds. Beyond the cursory glance, that same search included with the phrase "and celebrities"? produces millions of hits. So many of our entertainment icons—the untouchable rich and famous—can tell us what's up with being down. Where does their sadness end and ours begin?

I sometimes overlook my own grief by immersing myself in that of others. As a highly empathetic person, I know of no other way than to care for others. In my career as English and humanities faculty at the University of Wisconsin-Green Bay, I spend my nights and weekends wading through student angst and pain found in the safe harbor of creative writing—often, prompting to me to fill out reports for students of concern, or to at least send the message—"Thank you for trusting me with this. Are you okay?" I am concerned with their depression. Anxiety. Lack of sleep. Lack of appetite. Lack of energy. Lack of motivation. Lack of joy. The lack.

When I carve out my syllabi across every course I teach, from the basic Composition One equivalency to public speaking, I meticulously scour the earth to embed content addressing mental health. It is my hidden curriculum—my passion pedagogy. Because the Jurassic era "sage on the stage" methodology of teaching died a long time ago. Because it is my responsibility to students to guide and equip them—they are not going to give a damn about self- discovery, career-pathing, or any course content if they can't get out of bed.

This past year, I designed a course for a two-hundred level topics of literature course: Mental Health: from Madness to Mainstream, a survey course analyzing the depiction of mental health from Austen to Carver; Plath to Sexton; Nick Flynn's Another Bullshit Night in Suck City to Jenny Lawson's Furiously Happy. While students are analyzing the text under the scaffolding of literature, what I really want is for them to find themselves among the pages and to be able to better address their own battles within the comforting distance of character and plot analysis. With purpose and passion, I make space for mental health long before I teach any other content and curriculum. It is not only because I care deeply about my students, for I do, but it has proven to be necessity.

Students need a mental-health advocate long before they can care about the rhetoric of social media or how to write a hermit crab essay. Visibility and inclusion are necessary. These tenets are not woke—they are humanist. Only in the modern age is it considered radical to care about people, to believe that it is a basic human right to have access to the table. To live outside of fear. Because everything now comes with what feels like a lifetime guarantee of false binary. Who wouldn't be depressed by that?

Across my courses, I am eternally seeking relevance and relation to anchor my students' learning experience to what is known; given the content, we frequently look to celebrity and pop culture. So many of our contemporary athletic and entertainment icons have given voice to their mental health; they've spoken the breath of truth into the previous career-stopping taboo of being unwell. Traditionally, society has had no place for our look-to's to be flawed; the audacity of being human, of being vulnerable, of succumbing to substance or sadness—or both. While there still are those who shame Simone Biles for "giving up" at the Olympics as she battled mental demons which quite literally could have broken her neck had she not set a boundary, there is a much larger army who support the human upon the podium of perfection we've placed her and all other celebrities on.

One celebrity journey in particular has been on my mind recently: child actress Drew Barrymore made her first break as a five-year-old; seven years later, she was an addict. This, while the rest of us Gen X-ers were glued to the walls of the gymnasium at the something-something dance, as the gym teacher DJ spun The Jets "Crush on You." There we were, bangled and tweeny, hormones revving, and America's 80's sweetheart was at Studio 54 doing lines of coke—our cherub E.T. girl with nose candy stuck to the appendages of her face.

By age 13, her mother hastily institutionalized the troubled teen at Van Nuys Psychiatric Hospital in Los Angeles, a well-known hard-core mental illness facility of padded cells and tie-ups; the details mirror "Hotel California"—some never leave. After a year and a half, she finally did. Arguably, this painful period was the catalyst which pushed her to emancipate from her parents at age fourteen.

In the years since, Barrymore has been very open about her time at the institution and even made a televised, teary, yet triumphant return to the haunt in 2021. While Van Nuys is no longer in operation, it left an indelible scar on its patients, to which Drew was not exempt. Suicidal ideation continued beyond her time there and well into the next two decades.

I had no idea. What do you mean our eternal "it girl" was living in her own apartment while I was busy lamenting some elusive tinsel-toothed junior football player who had the unmitigated gall to flirt with but reject me? I was a sad, angsty-teenager; not unlike Drew, I too, had a stint in a facility which did me no damn good. I was never restrained—I never needed to be. I just smoked older teens' cigarettes, flirted too much with the idea of being older than I was, and wore too much Aqua Net. I wasn't criminally "master, cut away the stone of folly" insane—I was fucking depressed—not a very revolutionary concept regarding a teenager.

In reality, substance abuse is to depression is to anxiety is to grief. The vessels are different, but the lamentations are the same. Like music, suffering is universal. The 1990's were a Hollywood blur for Drew—movies and money and several romantic engagements ending in nowhere. In 2012 she found the man who would become the father of her two children; they were divorced four years later. This is when the pain descended most, and Barrymore took to swimming through vats of alcohol to self-anesthetize.

How is this possible? How can one be a modern Shirley Temple but still miserable? Much of Barrymore's mental health can easily be attributed to the pressure of the white-hot spotlight. It was not enough to be thrust onto the Hollywood scene as a five-year-old, then making her big break three years later as Gertie in E.T.. She went on to be cast in a number of starring roles from Firestarter to Never Been Kissed. This success wasn't enough to quiet the internal storm. Somewhere in Josie Grossy's pain of isolation and rejection, we see that the vein of self- doubt runs deeper than method-acting. Then came Adam Sandler, the golden-touch protagonist, and we fell in love with the 80's duo in The Wedding Singer. We love them again, differently, and repeatedly, six years later in 50 First Dates.

Along came a masterpiece of Barrymore's acting portfolio—a Golden Globe winning portrayal of Edith "Little Edie" Bouvier Beale in 2009's Grey Gardens; a remake of the reclusive mother-daughter documentary filmed in the mid-1970's. But one also wonders how much of a stretch it was for her— a wealthy, public-spotlight reduced to reclusive and roof-feeding raccoons. Little Edie was a fascinating and complex woman; no doubt, a cathartic experience for Drew to believably pull the part off—so much so that she, herself, withdrew on set to remain in character. Undoubtedly, she had decades of stifling the silence of suffering to keep her "in there" as Little Edie—flawlessly delivering with the exact inflection as Beale herself, "It's very difficult to keep the line between the past and the present. You know what I mean? It's awfully difficult."

Arguably, Drew was at the pinnacle. It still wasn't enough, as up to this point, she battled numerous bouts of depression and suicidal ideation. Two decades after the start of her burgeoning career, in the open-address of her own television talk show, she shares about her heavy drinking problem after divorce in 2016. This rock-bottom came with an even higher price tag—that which likely pushed her towards a renewed commitment to sobriety—her own therapist broke up with her. They reconciled when Drew was sober again in 2019. She is still sober, and the very lightness in her being is her two children, but the dossier and dollar signs she's earned don't hurt.

Since the mid 2000's, Drew found her way through unfiltered chaos; an impressive film and TV portfolio as actress and producer, a book, and break-out as host of her own TV show where she unapologetically tackles everything from mental health to the stigma of menopause. She's got a healthy lineup of entrepreneurial market-corners including partnerships with sustainable cleaning products (Flower), her own makeup line, and now… cookware—in all of it, color and joy. Laugh out loud, head thrown back, open-mouthed, unabashed Barrymore joy. The darkness has left the building. It is possible to walk through the fire, maintain the scars on your feet, and still regularly paint and pedicure whatever you have left. Laugh at the bewilderment of childhood stardom, the fall from grace, and the ascent to a net worth of 130 million.

If only everything were infused with that much redemption. Aunt Carol, across the bay, has now been fighting MS, Lung cancer, and brain cancer, but the universe threw in COVID-19 and pneumonia a few days ago. It will be the pneumonia which takes her—any day now, I'm told. Reader, in the three weeks it's taken me to episodically write this, Jack, my beloved adopted-Uncle, did indeed fail to thrive—he passed not of dementia but congestive heart failure. Carol is next. Again the grief-drift rises in my chest—him, him, her— lifetime lover, father, sister. Brian. Dad. Rachel.

Seven years ago, at the end of the season of goodbye-for-now's, I did not care if I lived or not. I was not suicidal, but I was in no great rush to find a reason not to pass away. That is, up until the moment I was diagnosed with a brain aneurysm, (which claimed my sister) and ironically, I chose to fight back. I know grief like I know if I'm running a fever. If a man finds me attractive. If a dog wants a treat. I know grief.

It's been two days; Aunt Carol flew away this morning. She hung on long enough to watch the Michigan State/Ohio University game. She watched football until she no longer was. I will teach and I will write (or not) and I will march through the days as I am expected to while coming to terms with what unintentionally defines me at every turn to those who see me beyond a cursory creature—tragedy is to my core. Like Barrymore, however, I fight for the joy. I insist on it to the point of defiance.

What is greatly ironic to me, even now, having spent decades wondering if the warm lighting inside well-landscaped homes speaks truth to the experience of the walls within—if what we perceive is true and glitter is in fact gold? Celebrity is not above humanity. Nor vulnerability. Nor frailty. The very fact that I spent my first 20 years looking longingly at other people who curated the narrative long before I knew what that meant is greatly ironic. So many, too many, have fallen. The pedestal we place others on, particularly celebrities, is not only based on our perception of their existence, but the structure we place them on is sedimentary. They are people sometimes at the end of themselves; other times, at the beginning of a new adventure.

After moving to a new home-for-now, and not yet finding the boxes I don't have the time to unpack, I found myself in a big box store buying the necessities of the first few days in a new home. There it was in the store; I stared stupidly. A frying pan. THE pan. Gray ceramic food-facing, black outside, gold handle; cursive wax-like stamp "B" for Barrymore brand Beautiful in the handle and the bottom of that glorious fry-baby.

A desolate heart drowned in addiction, remnants of two failed marriages, and at times a broken career, our 80's sweetheart found her way to a Beautiful life—stepped out of silver spoon chaos to cook with a golden handle. I'm not one for the transfer fallacy of celebrity endorsement, so I walked away to another aisle (returned minutes later to put the Black Sesame pan in my cart). I could buy two pans for the $20. I could… but other brands weren't forged in the same fire. They didn't come out willfully resilient. They didn't keep prospering solely by blind faith. They didn't choose joy despite every reason not to—despite the frequent seizing in their chests and the familiar "not again." We did.

It really is a beautiful pan.

Roshelle Amundson

Home for World-Weary Hearts

The first summer I lived in the city I compulsively collaged cardboard houses. It began because I live near a Greek Orthodox church that houses a mini shrine next to the sidewalk. The intricate carvings of this devotional dollhouse caught my eye as I walked to and from the train. When my roommate caught COVID, I took the opportunity to pay homage to the shrine. I cut copies of my own out of pizza boxes, painted them pink or black or blue and carefully selected images to cover the cardboard. These images were textures from knitted blankets, hand-patched clothes, leaves, flower petals, and hardwood floors. I chose figures of women with long dresses, large afros, and longing eyes. I cut out vases, curled up sleeping dogs, bed frames, and angels. Soon my apartment was filled with these little homes.

During those months everything fell off the walls, each frail piece of paper falling to the unrelenting blast of the air conditioner. Sometimes I would walk into a room to find the shrines laying on top of the magazine scattered floors. I would lean over in my clogs and desperately tack them back up. We resorted to pins to hold our colorful exhibition postcards, Students for a Democratic Society pamphlets, flyers for a friend of a friend's house show, protest signs for the overturning of Roe v. Wade, and a card from my mother. But there was always an empty spot on the wall in the kitchen where the collage that was each month's calendar (made during the last Friday of the following month by our party guests) should have rested. My roommate and I would turn to each other and say, "May falls away."

It was against this backdrop that my phone calls home to central Illinois progressively got more frantic.

****

When I dream of "home" my mind paints the picture of a particular farm in Scotland: fluffy goats in a muddy yard surround a small cobblestone house with a bright red roof, brighter than the pair of tiny yellow galoshes tossed in the yard. Inside the cottage there is a man sitting at a kitchen table with a notebook and a tall glass of foaming beer. A woman with straight yellow hair holding a baby looks sadly across the room at her husband. The same baby is in the accompanying photograph my mind has memorized on the topic. In it, the same man stands in the same yard and holds the tiny baby inside his shearling jacket; only her darling face is peeking out. Her name is Stella. The man is Paul McCartney.

The house is the setting where he conceived his second solo album, Ram, an album I, for the most part, ignored during my childhood Beatles obsession, until my dad showed me the song "Uncle Albert/Admiral Halsey." I would slouch with-

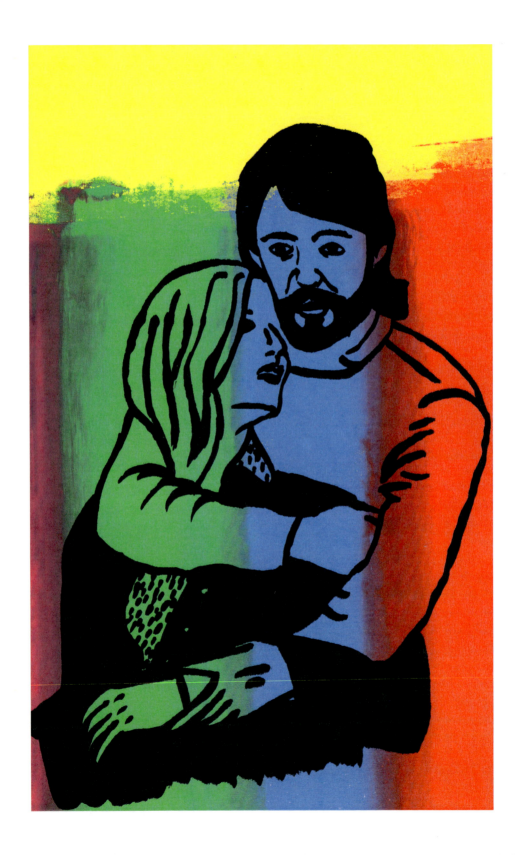

in my dining room's window seat and listen to its woven rainy-day soundscape through my headphones on my iPod Nano, the melodic refrains bouncing from ear to ear in stereo. Through the lyrics, Linda and Paul reached across the ocean to one another. Their love reached out to me, and I was hooked.

Ram is a sonic tapestry and a fertile field of collaboration "by: Paul McCartney and Linda McCartney." The "and Linda" to this project is key. Her vocals are omnipresent in the background. It's she who makes the food in the song "Eat at Home." She is the heart in "Heart of the Country." She is the "Long Haired Lady," the "love [he] finds… awake and waiting for me." Ram is a love letter to Linda that she got to cowrite. I'm blown away when I think how much he loved her to want to share his artmaking process with her. He didn't want her to be his muse but his collaborator. What sort of love would it be to respect one another so much; to be husband and wife is one thing, but to share the public eye as collaborators is to merge the personal with the produced.

Ram is pure homegrown art goodness. Paul tries out bluesy guitars and writes of walking a horse up a hill as the couple experiments with growing their own vegetables. He combines the witty ditties of his English heritage with the country sound of Linda's Americanness. Expertly layered harmonic vocals from the two of them croon on the track "Dear Boy" such simple sweet (slightly cautionary) lyrics to the effect of a symphony. "Monkberry Moon Delight" could be a nursey rhyme except it's accompanied by some seriously skilled blues piano and Paul's gritty yelling. He writes songs with childish imagination and funny rhymes as he helps raise Linda's daughter and a baby of their own.

Somehow Ram was panned critically when it came out. Rolling Stone famously bashed it. It was seen as unfinished, sloppy, nonsensical, and wishy-washy. The technical skill music critics of the future would praise was described at the time as trick work which couldn't back up the album's "lack of substance." Ringo Starr said the album made him think "Paul has gone wacky."

The more I read about the Ram album era the more I realized it wasn't a time of happily ever after. Paul went through a period of alcoholism. There was legal trouble, an effect of the internationally grieved Beatles breakup. A breakup which was the result of festering hurt feelings between men who used to be brothers. And so, Paul ran away to the county with his family. We must think of the magic of Ram, home, and partnership as the fallout from the breakup of the most famous rock band in the world.

****

When I find myself thinking about homes, I play a grainy technicolor film of Paul and Linda's farm in my mind. I think of the line in "Too Many People:" "Too many people sharing party lines/Too many people never sleep-in late/Too many people paying parking fines/Too many hungry people losing weight." I pay half of the rent which increases each year. I read about the mayor tearing down a tent settlement built by houseless people right as November begins. The same winter I took a course entitled: "Globalization and Narratives of U.S Decline." The first two weeks of which I took from my bed because in-person classes were cancelled due to the pandemic.

When I think of home, I think of the bright orange building in the vacant lot which will soon be the National Public Housing Museum. Last fall semester each Friday afternoon I had the good fortune of attending a museum class taught by the executive director, Lisa Lee.

I sat in the cold college classroom, wrapped in my bulky coat, and watched my professor Lisa lecture on museums. She would walk back and forth in front of the room in go-go boots, transforming the class's idea of museums and speaking of "theories of change," how she hopes the museum they are building will "illuminate dignity" for a population (public housing residents) our country has stereotyped. We believed her. We want to live in a world different than the one where a former President coined the term "welfare queen." The building where the museum will be is an original public housing unit built after the Second World War. One of the units in the museum will be a reproduction of a Jewish family's apartment from that postwar period. To that family, a home of their own meant their first Kosher kitchen. Another apartment will be a reproduction of an African American family from the 70's. The woman who lived there said her mother only bought a TV to hear Martin Luther King Jr. speak.

Lisa showed us plans for the music room, the exhibits of former residents' favorite items (with labels written by them, not curators), and the oral history library. She told us how the building will also have 15 units of housing (1/3 will be public, 1/3 affordable housing, and 1/3 priced at market). Lisa spoke of the museum as an intermedium salon, as a political organizing space, as a home, as a path to the future. When I looked at these building plans, I saw hope.

****

It is March 2012, and I am turning 10 years old. I'm hanging upside down from my twin sized bed. My upside-down gaze is pointed at the cracked ceiling of my 1911 house, fixated specifically on the glow-in-the-dark stars a little girl my age placed in 1990. Enter my mom, laundry basket balanced on one hip and in her other hand my birthday present: a CD wrapped in colorful funny pages. I unwrap it and meet eyes with a woman with curly frizzy hair (just like mine!) in a pair of worn flared jeans sitting barefoot in a curtain-shadowed window seat. A cat looms in the fuzzy foreground. "This album was everywhere when I was a kid," my mom explains uncharacteristically shy. "It meant the world to me." Tapestry by Carole King would have a monumental impact on me as well. Two months later I presented a report on it to my 5th grade class.

Carole wrote Tapestry after moving to Laurel Canyon to get away from a cheating husband. After completing the divorce (a taboo move at the time), she found herself not only without a husband but without a songwriting partner. The two of them had made a slew of radio hits in the 60's. Nevertheless, his absence was not detrimental. Laurel Canyon was the place to be. In my head, I place it parallel to Paris in the early 20's. Gertrude Stein is Mama Cass. Hemingway is Jim Morrison. Yeah, something like that. Anyway, Carole King left New York and found a bustling new creative community She began a lifelong collaboration with James Taylor (so good a friend that he made famous her composition "You've Got a Friend," which is also featured on Tapestry). She collaborated with Toni Stern, who wrote many of the lyrics on the album. She crafted Tapestry surrounded by musician friends like Taylor, Joni Mitchell, and Danny Kortchmar.

Tapestry is beautiful, strong, and vulnerable. This gift from my mother taught me how to be a woman. Tapestry aligns in my mind with "the personal is political" tenement of second wave feminism. Track after track Carole longs for the idea of home not in a housewife way but in a human way. In "Where You Lead," "Home Again," and "Way Over Yonder," we see home reimagined as a NY apartment, friendly phone call, road trip or picket fence. Carole sings of being left behind in "So Far Away," going against the nomad lifestyle totted in her popular culture. She writes with honesty about relationships in a way pop had never seen from a single woman before. In "It's Too Late," "something has died inside" that she "can't hide or fake" so she stays "in bed all morning just to pass the time." She is gently insecure in front of a one-night stand in "Will You Love Me Tomorrow?" yet resolves in another song to "wake up with a smile on your face and show the world all the love in your heart."

With Tapestry, Carole became the first woman to win multiple Grammys, sweeping up best record, album, and song of the year. On a technical level she combined R&B, gospel, and folk influences all while manning the piano center stage, effectively inventing the singer-songwriter genre as we now know it.

****

Tapestry and Ram sit in my mind alongside other cultural pieces from the 70's: wood paneling, the obsession with macrame, and Hollie Hobby in her pioneer hat. The story often goes that this trend towards an earthy home was a backlash against the radical decade which came before it. Setting aside the influence of environmentalism, it generally goes that this fashion was pedaling domesticity to counteract the radical and progressive times. To this associative jump I plant my feet in the street and say: "No way!" Sure, the fashionable radical as a trend was dying. Former hippies morphed into Reagan voters. Ultimate housewife Phyllis Schlafly weaponized the home to push back the Equal Rights Amendment. But I will not relinquish the home to conservatives.

This is what I want to tell you: there's something about my perception of Paul loving Linda in that muddy farmhouse in Scotland. There's something revolutionary about Lisa's museum. There's something about Carole clinging to her tapestry as she remakes her home as a single woman. And there's something about leaving home after lockdown.

That something is that to be human is to want a home filled with love. When I think of all of those multicolored threads of longing and love I get up and open my front door.

Homemaking is a radical act that goes hand in hand with the cutting edge of political theory. Home is the setting in which dreams for the future are made. If it's not written at home, it's written from a place where one is wishing for home. When we praise art about houses and homes, we understand the "radical" idea that housing is a human right. When we find ourselves overwhelmed at the thought of our world aligning more and more with the late-stage capitalism; it is then we go home.

We go home not to surrender but to roost in a nest of love and creativity from which we can change the world.

Erin Boyle

The Letter I Never Wrote
—After a friend urged me to write the revered poet

Dear Dr. Angelou:

We have not formally met but I saw you on the evening of March 3, 1993 from across the auditorium of the Savage Hall at the University of Toledo. The Black Student Union welcomed you and the wisdom of your words: the poetic and inclusively kind.

In the ebony swell of thunderous praise you took your place, standing with purpose and dignity on a platform of yourself; regal and rising like poetry in motion. I was a face in a sea of witnesses experiencing the spirit of your strength. You possessed no hesitation or fear of fair-haired expectation but stood as a beautiful and phenomenal black woman commanding the space of respect that Aretha Franklin sang about.

I was in the room when it happened. The sound of a pin dropping was as eloquent as the signature of your song. It never skipped a beat. Your mic check was an original soundtrack in my ears.

How unabashed you sang against the backdrop of oppression. It sounded like the conviction of a choir, that acappella flow that makes knees want to bow and tongues confess. You surrendered your truth and the impact of your experiences.

You spoke as a witness with optimistic expectation, as if leaning over the highest balcony encouraging every race and creed to break bread of equal celebration. To pass the basket of love is a fruitful effort that serves not only ourselves but our brothers and sisters as well. You served us a full plate of your thoughts on the richness of our black history, and we hungered for more. But some politicians today have the audacity to say black folks made strides while our ancestors were enslaved in shackles. But my sister, we know better. The tribe of motherland arrived on America's soil equipped with skills before they sailed the middle passage, wordsmiths included.

You spoke about how our people carved a culture from the landmark of American history. After all, we uphold the banner of our black skin more than one month out of the year. The holiday is only a reminder, an observance of our everyday impact upon the landscape in America's story. Unfortunately, without it our achievements would be incessantly overlooked. Who can erase black history? Not even the governor of Florida. There are simply too many of us. Too many compelling stories that need to be told. Dr. Angelou, I believed you settled this in the spirit of your verse.

Nevertheless, your stage presence radiated the room like a river flowing with peace. Even the ecology of your thoughts sprung forth from the preservation of your record reminding me of your views on autobiography as an art form and the importance of memoirs. This form of storytelling has transformed my life by urging me to leave a legacy of my words.

Although I am not your daughter, I could be. I feel a kinship. We are partakers of prose, poetry, and playwriting. Doesn't that make us family of the craft? The influence of my work centers on my family and culture and speaks to a broader sense of community. There's something freeing and authentic about telling truth. The boldness of your words has encouraged me to write the vision. I have prayed while stepping out on faith and letting my voice find me. I too have found a community of sounds that lift my voice so I can sing.

It isn't often that a trailblazing star brings the warmth of conviction on a wintery day. I have witnessed you from my television screen and bookmarked the pages of your transparency. You left an impression. The first woman and the first African American to stand before dignitaries on a dais to perform poetry at the inauguration of former U.S. President Bill Clinton. Sister, with tenacity you handled your business and reclaimed your say. You carried our people with your hope. Your words inspired me to reflect upon who I am as a black woman and live in the rhythm of the sunrise, to stretch my mind with a plume in hand, poised from the black well of thought to create my own poetic justice. To be invited to America's table is the evidence of change born from being told to eat in the kitchen.

Some three decades later, Amanda Gorman, a young woman, and the third African American to perform the presidential inaugural poem. You would have been proud to watch her work. But livid to learn that her poem had been banned from some Florida school due to a parent's protest. How disrespectful for Amanda's book, The Hill We Climb, to be relegated to a dusty corner of a school library just because it garnered too much attention.

You are the most banned author in the United States because you advocate for those imprisoned birds. I remember devouring the pages of your book, and dog-earing the profound and worthy passages for me to return to. How can anyone disregard the challenge of words from a revered writer who has strained and suffered through the midnight oil? Perhaps there is some fear-based ideology that someone else will get the upper hand and simply tell the truth.

Sometimes people just refuse to read and discount what is raw and provocative. I found your coming-of-age story relegated to a waste bin nearly twenty years ago. But I dumpster dived to reclaim its pocketed grace. Dusted off its neglect and gave it a new home.

Perhaps I'm preaching to the choir, but black autobiographies and other tomes should not have to ache where they are not appreciated. Still, they rise and make their presence known. For every black narrative outlawed I stand and homeschool my own mind. And as I discover new things around me, I pass on that knowledge to others. Professor Angelou, I do believe you are still teaching. We may not have control over every unsavory morsel the world serves up, but we can certainly advocate for what matters and not be curtailed by the clamor of racism. Unfortunately, there are political structures, even now desiring to bag the fruit of black bodies. The evidence is in the falling trees.

In my early twenties, I found another collection of your poetry, bound in orange and gold. Someone had the audacity to place the sass and say-so of your phenomenal words in the lost and found. But I retrieved its perfection in the palm of my hands; turned every page of its dazzling constellation. After all, one man's junk is another's treasure.

Perhaps you think my pen is just rambling in its ink, but this long letter is all the conversations we should have had. A dear friend suggested that I write to you years ago. I just get caught up.

Maya, I understand I do not have the freedom to call you by your first name; it isn't out of disrespect, but to pay you homage. The sound of your name flows like a song worthy of singing. The way your brother Bailey pronounced it became stuck in my mind like well-informed volumes. I know better than to call you by your first name. I was raised to address my elders by titles such as, Mr., Mrs., Ms., Dr., Sir, or Ma'am.

I know folks were stirred up about your response to the girl who addressed you by your first name on national television. You schooled her with sound advice to call you Dr. Angelou. I get it. You have lived a long life and command respect. No one has the authority to call you by your first name unless you give them permission to do so. Our elders have given themselves and have a rightful place to spread their purpose in this life. After all, they are not "sacks on a shelf."

My mother and grandmother poured their light into my drinking gourd so I would not become thirsty, complacent, or lost during my journey as a black woman. I am not a mutation of racial intolerance, nor am I a performance of anyone's colorblindness; an invisible version of themselves. I am powered up and "tangled up knowing how I got over from the middle passage to poetry."

I admire your sense of grace and unswerving narrative. At the University you spoke with a poet's precision. You said what you meant to say and meant what you said. As a poet I have been known to compare myself to other poets. In my spirit, I can hear you telling me to be inspired by reading my own work to stimulate my creative juices. And in doing so, it feels like letting the sun shine on my significance as its very presence douses every shadow and shape of doubt that hampers my progress. Your words have encouraged me to sit with my own words, speak with my ears and let them continuously be open to conversations.

For me, you are a star flickering in the breadth of a black sky of sequins from galaxies away. When I look up, I see your light still burning. I challenge myself that no matter how daunting the second, third, or twentieth rejection I receive when sending my poetry out into the world, I still need to send it. So, thank you for bringing light from the dark corners of your world.

Although a thief stole your diamonds he was captured by a cold grave. I say, let the buried stay buried in the past. But you know how history has a way of unearthing itself. There is power in your tongue, and the silences of your truth are golden lessons for anyone willing to receive it. This is where flowers bloom and endure the sun and the rain. I may not have experienced your specific suffering, but I've had folks wield their words against me like smooth criminals, and some version of their scenario begins to leak from my ink of pen into a poem. So in that vein, I can say we both have fought back with our literary insight.

There is no shame in your game, the way you set the stage of your voice for my listening. If I'm not being too forward, I read somewhere you were not comfortable in marriages to white men due to racism in America. But today racism still lives and breathes like Goliaths we must constantly slay. I too, am a black woman living in America in an interracial marriage, but I have learned to address microaggressions from those on the outside looking in. Besides, who can fit into my experience? My shoes are simply not the right size for their journey, and they can never walk all those miles I have accumulated.

I always knew you were a world traveler. You have been to Africa and stayed in the homes of many distinct faces. Wherever you are, you seem to feel at home cooking up the flavor of gratitude. Though I am not a globetrotter, your astute point of view encourages me to grow wherever I am planted.

As a poet and black woman, you still rock because you found ways to discover your voice and navigate the black experience while witnessing the cradle of life rattling with celebration. You survived with grace and faith, that barren place where Jim Crow cawed with the brashness to say you were not even first rate to breathe the air of advantage. But you inhaled it anyway. The sound of your sass is as eloquent as a bird taking flight.

I had every intention of posting this note years ago, after I saw you on stage, but the notion ran off like butter melting over good grits; I left the table before I had the opportunity to consume them. I got in my own way and let this letter languish in a dusty notebook and a folder full of unfinished poems until I listened to your Master Class. This is me knowing better than to procrastinate because of any fear of failing. I know now that faith finances my journey.

If you haven't figured it out yet, my writing has been informed by your formidable approach to life by taking the common and everyday and reworking it to allow the reader to reflect and learn something refreshing. This concept reverberates daily in my spirit.

We have composed our own worlds, yet we have never properly met. You are a renaissance woman: a daughter, sister, mother, friend, wife, professor, playwright, memoirist, and creator; a performer, historiographer, a filmmaker, and an activist. As black women we wear hats that fit us for numerous occasions. It is our way of advancing ourselves.

I can almost hear a train whistling in Stamps, Arkansas. Your arrival on the scene of your youth, stepped from a railcar with luggage tags swinging on your arms like lucky charms. Sometimes as children we do not acquire everything we desire in life, but we somehow gather what is essential for our survival. You did that! A strong black woman does not need anyone's permission to tell her how to live her life or express herself.

Dr. Angelou, when you gave a keynote speech, you gave all you had, and it came back to you in good measure, pressed down, shaken together, and running over. The performance of your voice was like a choir singing an A & B selection with an encore. You bestowed upon us your harmony, power, and the art of a griot. I follow you, not on Facebook, Instagram, Twitter; I simply read your legacy.

Although my shyness did not climb from the bleachers to meet you that day in 1993, I wanted to introduce myself, tell you I was a poet too. I wanted to take my paper origami of verses, press them into your seasoned palms for you to read. And in my mind, you'd smile that broad smile and say, "Sister, you've got potential."

I can almost hear warm laughter, with the echo of your voice through all your platforms urging me to step from my comfort zone, beyond every circumstance to become the writer I am meant to be.

Some stars let go of fear by taking a leap of faith and breaking through the dense stratosphere just to burn their flame. They seek the highest canopy from which their gleam is held brightly.

Dr. Angelou, when you rose upon that stage many years ago something rose up in me. Though I am older and wiser, I am "taking up time and space," to post this letter today. To stand upon your shoulders is to learn to shine my own light and share it with others.

With Gratitude,
Sandra

Sandra Rivers-Gill

Spill Into Everything, No Longer Ignoring Grief

At thirty years old, I find myself having a midlife crisis.

"But why, Coe? You're so young!"

Stop kidding yourself. If I lived to sixty, it would be a miracle.

I've concluded it's a midlife crisis because the first half of my life is catching up to me—but not how I expected. Is that what a midlife crisis is? I think so.

I always envisioned my climacteric as a symphony of discontent echoing the classic femme archetype. A disenchanted dance, entangled in the woes of my career, haunted by the specter of wrinkles, and consumed by the worries of an emptying nest. And there, all the while, I would lay reclining on a chaise lounge, elegantly holding an opera-length cigarette holder with ash that would make Shelly DuVall green with envy.

No. In reality, I find myself in a collective period of mourning.

Now, I wasn't oblivious to my sorrow. I was simply too busy to grieve. Always the caretaker, I've spent my life hopping from one trauma to another to keep a roof over my (and my loved ones) heads. So I kept putting it off. Later, later, later.

I didn't know I'd ignored grief for so long that it would spill into everything. But then, it crashed like a wave of blood in the Stanley Hotel lobby.

But what was the catalyst? What finally tipped the scales, unzipping everything I'd worked so hard to compartmentalize?

It was Xiu Xiu's shadowy creation, Ignore Grief. Though I had listened to it when it was released in March of this year, its weight and significance eluded me until a month later. But it was only a matter of time before I caught up with the whispers of my own heart. Delayed, but not denied.

The irony of my tardy awakening! Yet, despite the delay, its impact remained profound. The album became an agent of change, unraveling the fabric of my reality and exposing my neglected fragments.

Ignore grief? How could I any longer?

Yet, this awakening was not without its challenges, and this isn't a piece dick-riding Jamie Stewart and Angela Seo (even though I would happily do so and 100% slipped my number in a business email to the former.)

(Sorry.)

Like the coffee spilled in the Ikea elevator, grief seeped into every nook and cranny, demanding to be acknowledged and dealt with.

I felt naked, exposed.

Alone.

I still do.

The sticky mess on a stranger's shoe.

(I have to be mopped up.)

So, for the first time, I muster the courage to confront the daunting list of things I'm actively grieving. It's an inventory of the palpable losses collected over the years, silently weighing upon my spirit.

As I voice these unspoken sorrows, they materialize before me, demanding and receiving the space they deserve. Consider it a last-ditch effort to mop me up, my "Green Onion" two-minute sweeping scene.

I grieve for my parents, who I've become more like than I ever knew possible.
I grieve for every unfinished plate of food I left behind.
I grieve for the opportunities I had to spit on a man and didn't.
I grieve for the songs I didn't sing—at karaoke, in the car, on my own.
I grieve for the vicenarian who never got to experience the best of being a twenty-something.
I grieve for the family heirlooms I've had to leave in the basements of abandoned houses.
I grieve for the friends I never met.
I grieve for the friends I did meet but am estranged from.
I grieve for not going to California.
I grieve for the words left unsaid.
I grieve for the little girl who walked home covered in Mountain Dew.
I grieve for my collections, sold off and taken away.
I grieve for the queer who was closeted far too long.
I grieve for the car I totaled when I drove it off the cliff.
I grieve for my body, which still holds the trauma from when I drove it off the cliff.
I grieve for the children he curated.

This is not a journey towards healing or closure—it is an exhumation of buried emotions, a confrontation with irretrievable losses that shape my very being. I am marked by these griefs, etched with the scars of what could have been.

But I find a strange liberation in this mournful dance with my existence. Embracing our sorrows, and recognizing their power over us, allows us to understand ourselves and the intricate tapestry of human experience.

So, I'll ignore grief no longer. Instead, I'll take its hand and pull it close, for in its embrace lies the key to unlocking profound truths and embracing the unvarnished reality of who I am.

Coe Collette

Marilyn Monroe Dies; Pills Blamed

INT - *Bedroom.*

Title Card: *12305 Fifth Helena Drive, Brentwood, CA. August 5th, 1962. Iris in. Extreme long shot into a small, modest bedroom from outside the window.*

Title Card: *Marilyn bought this house four months ago, purchased at the request of her psychiatrist. She was born as Norma, named after silent film star Norma Talmadge. She only changed it to Marilyn because she was told it better suited her for Hollywood.*

High angle, peering through squared wooden muntins. Glass softens the view. Establishing shot of room. White walls and white carpet, white sheets and white blankets. The colored comforter breaks the pattern, glazed and silky as it reflects light from a nearby lamp with a crooked shade.

Pan right. A plastic hanger rests on the lid of a bureau. Clothes dangle over the edges of both. An expensive fur shawl, sleek and black, is clumsily balled up and tossed beside the mess.

Title Card: *Marilyn's inspiration was rooted in silent films. So much so, she impersonated Theda Bara as an homage during a photoshoot. Both women were sex symbols of their eras, bringing a sensuality to their acting that encouraged change in conservative media. Marilyn's movies might have had sound, but many of them were still in the gritty black and white film that Theda worked with.*

Pan left, steady. Packages and purses are piled up by the closed door on the adjacent wall. A mirror is nestled behind them to keep it upright. Against the near wall with the window is a bed, which is nothing more than a mattress guarded by a fitted sheet atop a thick box spring.

Tilt down. There's a woman lying beneath the blankets, undisturbed.

Title Card: *No one has found her yet. No clock is there to tell the time, but it's late. After midnight. Other than the light still being on, the world could assume she was asleep.*

Pan further left, stay tilted down. Zoom to a close-up. Her body is tucked under the covers, nude beneath the silk. The comforter is hardly pulled past her hips, letting the camera glimpse a small bruise on the small of her back.

Title Card: *It's a bruise that will make people speculate her suicide as a murder for decades. Was she assassinated to keep an affair with John F. Kennedy quiet? Or was it the work of the CIA or the Mafia, because she knew something about the president's link to crime?*

Move back to a medium shot, still from outside the window. Tilt up. Her face is obscured, planted in plush pillows. Her blonde hair is messy and unstyled, an unusual choice for someone known for her beauty. No makeup, either. She would be left untouched by the police who would later enter the room, face bare until the service. Then, the artist she personally requested would do her makeup for the burial.

Title Card: A Frank Sinatra record had been on the turntable when police broke in through the window, needle frozen at the spindle. Marilyn had dated Sinatra, once. He gave her a little Maltese terrier named Maf, and he'd wanted to marry her. But he only wanted it before he realized that she couldn't be saved.

Close-up shot, tilt down. A telephone cord is snaked beneath the crack in her bedroom door, twisting all the way up into her grasp where there must have been a receiver hidden beneath her breasts.

Pan right to the bedside table, camera lens pressed up against the window. It is a messy little thing, teetering by the foot of Marilyn's makeshift bed rather than where tables like it would usually be. Empty bottles of prescription medication are scattered on and beneath it.

Title Card: *Those are the real villains of the story. A barbiturate called Nembutal was found during the autopsy to be at lethal levels. The coroner said she might have swallowed forty-seven pills of Nembutal, which hemorrhaged the lining of her stomach. Might because the world didn't want to believe she swallowed the cocktail of barbiturates in a single gulp. In the decades since, the media would spin webs of conspiracy, of murder, of assassination, which never had any grounding outside of pure speculation.*

Zoom back out, mid-shot. The side of her face is just visible from this angle, the one seen eye closed like she's nothing but asleep. Her cheeks have already lost the vivacious color it held before, veins bruised and purple beneath the skin.

Title Card: *Suicides peaked across the globe after news of her death hit the papers. New York saw twelve in one day. A note left by one victim read: "If the most wonderful, beautiful thing in the world has nothing to live for, then neither must I."*

Long shot, then extended long shot. The room is quiet, bathed in black and white like the evidence pictures of it will later be. The Sinatra record has long since clicked to a stop.

Title Card: *Around four in the morning, the housekeeper will notice the light beneath the door. She'll try the door, and when Marilyn doesn't answer, she'll call the police and help Marilyn's psychiatrist break through the bedroom window. It's too late to be useful, and she knows it. When police arrive, she'll be doing laundry in an untroubled, quiet way. She's given up hope before she* *even sees Marilyn dead.*

Iris out.

Emma Snyder

Girls like Girls: the Revolutionary Reverie of Hayley Kiyoko

It was December 2015 when I discovered Hayley Kiyoko, or rather when Hayley Kiyoko helped rediscover me beneath a bloodied face, as I shed heavy tears on a lonely dorm room floor. But let me circle back.

The prior year I had worked arduously in Berlin to earn a full scholarship to go abroad and study musicology at a liberal arts college in Portland, Oregon, an enchanted little place with Tudor-Gothic brick buildings that were proudly marked with commemorative plates attesting they were a century old. They were embedded in a beautiful canyon and formed their own highly contained human ecosystem. It was what I wanted after a tragic love affair with a girl in the urban jungle that is Berlin—a girl unable to come to terms with the fact that the person she loved happened to be a girl, too. I thought that maybe in a college bubble as tiny and dreamy as this one, people wouldn't be able to lie, hide, and disappear as easily as in a European capital. Maybe, if I could unravel the realities of the USA, that country that exists more than any other on glimmering film gauge in real life, I would be able to unravel the complicated reality of me.

I did not arrive in the best condition. I carried with me a broken heart, the deep wounds of a shattered family, and the litany of binaries that made up the sum of me to many people: biracial, bisexual, brought up Christian while being queer. Frankly, I was already tired of a lifetime trying to reconcile any of them. I was resolute to avoid further heartbreak in this new beginning far from home—my focus was to be on my studies, making new friends, and to absolutely avoid anything that might escalate into romance.

Naturally, I fell in love an embarrassing three weeks later and when it happened my entire mind was screaming ABORT in four languages. I remained steadfast for a about a week in trying to keep her at a distance. Like me she was part Latina, had already lived in multiple countries, and was brought up with Christianity and rigorous expectations of what it meant to be female. Unlike me she was still in absolute denial of her sexuality. It screamed powder keg of galactic proportions, and I attempted valiantly to keep from lighting its fuse.

But she latched onto me the minute she heard my curious Spanish. When we exited our shared class, she walked backwards in front of me in her self-painted Doc Martens, asking me a thousand things in a melodious rapid fire and with a glimmering cigarette in the corner of her mouth, her green eyes sparking my every sense. Finally, she pulled the cigarette from her lips and put it between mine with a serious crease between her brows. "I want to ask you questions," she declared in Spanish, with a sincerity that tore down all defenses of my heart for good.

Two months in a lavender haze of innocent discovery and overwhelming passion, one month of hard realities and wrestling identities, and another month of helpless implosion and her hand in the paw of the most obnoxious macho on campus later, I returned to my dorm room after a night of mad dancing, drinking, and finally smashing my face into an ancient oak tree with an agonized scream. I sunk down to the floor, pressed my bleeding, heated face into the cold tiles, and finally allowed myself to cry. You should have known, I told myself angrily, over and over again, feeling like the biggest fool on earth. I couldn't tell you how long I lay there, honestly—my phone was chiming with worried inquires by the friends I had left when I'd fled into the stillness of the canyon without warning. The incessant pings died down by the time my tears had finally run out and I took in the dead silence of the room, feeling blissfully empty for the mercy of a second. Then, another loud ping and everything flooded back. I groaned and aggressively pulled my phone to my face, only to laugh when I saw a YouTube notification on top of a plethora of unread messages. It read: Watch: Girls like Girls by Hayley Kiyoko.

Girls like girls. The audacious simplicity of that title was like a genial spring shower on my battered self. "Not that easy, Hayley Kiyoko, not that fucking easy" I muttered to myself. I had never heard of her before, and who knows why I got that notification—the YouTube algorithm works in mysterious ways. But still, I wanted to know how that stranger would present her confident statement and sinking back onto the tiles I wiped the blood and tears from my eyes and pressed play.

The girl who opened the video—the credits would name her as Coley—rode a yellow bike on heat-cracked American asphalt, and eerily enough she had blood and bruises on her face, too. She was beautiful and forlorn, a mist of fate surrounding her. She rode up to an expensive-looking suburban house and knocked on a door, which was opened by another stunning girl with Asian features (Sonya) who looked at Coley with unconcealed elation. When we cut back to our heroine, who greets her friend with loving adoration in her eyes, her face is clear of blood -the opening was a flash-forward.

A strange excitement gripped me as I sat up, my muscles hurting and me paying them no mind as I grabbed my phone with both hands. And so, I watched the video that would change me and millions of others for the very first time. As an aspiring filmmaker, I quickly noticed its high production value: the creamy California colors and sun-washed dream aesthetics. Falling into its story you could smell sunscreen, melted asphalt, orange trees, and the strawberry-flavored lipstick the girls painted on each other with aching tenderness. I watched, mouth agape, as scenes of my life unfolded right there on the tiny screen: the sexual tension of sharing a cigarette only to look away shyly? Being mesmerized by the girl you loved dancing without music but making your heartstrings break into a full-out violin concerto on speed? Watching helplessly as she tolerated being pawed by a boy who regarded her like a pretty thing he owned, after she spent two hours caressing your face through the acceptable but highly sensual touch of a lipstick to your mouth?

I had lived all these scenes but had never seen them on film before. Not in the shape of a 35mm dream, at least not without turning into male gaze exploitation or tragic death, Hollywood's favorite ending for people like us. With a start I remembered the blood on Coley's face in the beginning of the video and I braced myself for the inevitable dreadful ending. But wait—this music sounded like a happy pop song and my brain was thoroughly confused.

Sure enough, the reverie gets pierced with harsh reality when the girls are finally about to kiss and Sonya's boyfriend appears and brutally smashes Coley into a row of rocks. And as Coley lies bleeding on the ground while the assaulter screams at a terrified Sonya, and I resigned myself to the inevitable punitive ending... Coley gets up and fights back.

Now that was a scene I definitely had never seen before. The beginning? Of course. I bear the scar reminders of the Colombian men who discovered my 'sin' and can still feel the kicks to my head and stomach. Had I wanted to hit them back? Yes. Had I dared to do it? No. In the end reality teaches us that fighting back violent men untrained rarely ends well. But seeing that unlikely scenario, a queer girl triumphantly defending herself in a music video? It was heart stopping.

Unsurprisingly, once Girls like Girls went viral, there were plenty 'concerned' straight viewers who pointed to that scene as glamorizing violence, conveniently ignoring who started it. Many excused the boys' attack, for hadn't the girl not almost kissed his property girlfriend in front of him? It fit into a handy stereotype people have of women who love women: the angry dyke. One of the most common terms in my native German for gay women is Kampflesbe, literally: fight lesbian. People who use it sure claim ignorance to the fact that queer girls rarely start a fight like this, that most often they have to defend themselves from physical assault by men, only to be left bleeding on the floor of an uncaring police station. But Girls like Girls does not glamorize fighting violent men back. It happens quickly and off screen, not a drop of blood to be seen and Sonya hastily pulls Coley away. It was merely a part of the strikingly honest debut of Hayley Kiyoko's most powerful objective: showing the sweet yearning dreams and darker vengeance fantasies we all have at some point in our lives, but that queer girls were never entitled to without being called disgusting and predatory—nor without being punished by narrative death.

That was the ending I expected for Girls like Girls with good reason; the perpetual narrative of queer female characters who get brutally murdered moments after finding happiness was a trope so dominant that by 2015 it was known by a chilling name: Bury your gays. By the time Hayley's music video premiered the death toll of lesbian characters was so high that queer women finally had enough: the #wedeservebetter movement emerged in the same year, an unprecedented global outcry to bring to light the crushing psychological damage of perpetuating the deeply entrenched message that women who love women have to be punished and calling for its end.

Was it coincidental that this movement took off right after young Coley stood up to this grim fate in a viral pop music video? Would it have happened without the triumphant juxtaposition that was the string of songs and music videos Hayley Kiyoko wrote and directed right after? Videos that showed queer girls and women being in love, being shy, being outcast, being brave, and being flawed – in short, being fully fledged human beings allowed to make mistakes to the soundtrack of happy pop beats? I don't think so.

Change tends to happen when the camel's back finally breaks as a hopeful sun appears on the horizon. And in 2015 the rainbow camel had been broken thoroughly through a millennia, and Hayley Kiyoko rose as the trail blazer of that powerful new message, wrapped in California dreams: We deserve better. For not only does Coley fight back in Girls like Girls; she and Sonya get a happy ending. After a passionate kiss she rides off into the sunset with a blissful smile on her bloodied face and by the credits I was scrambling to Wikipedia with a speed that I promise would absolutely dazzle you.

Up until 2015, Hayley Kiyoko, the daughter of a Canadian figure skater of Japanese ancestry and an American comedian, was known mostly as an actress, appearing in a number of successful films such as Lemonade Mouth and Scooby-Doo! The Mystery Begins. But even when she played one of the most iconic queer-coded characters of all time, Velma Dinkley, in real life she was terrified of coming out as a lesbian, like most closeted young women are. As a biracial one in the show business? Only a fool would have told her to go for it back then.

So, at the beginning of her musical career, Kiyoko kept the straight facade by being part of an all-girls pop band, The Stunners, who even toured with Justin Bieber at the height of his fame. Kiyoko credits the heavy burden of being untruthful in her music and the success of the mega hit I kissed a Girl by Katie Perry for her decision to leave the public closet through a song more honest and heartfelt than any she had written before. Girls like Girls was to serve as her directorial debut and a dreamy and highly cinematic coming out, a project that would end up causing a global generation of girls to see themselves represented in way they had never experienced before. To date it has been streamed 150 million times and has been certified gold by the Recording Industry Association of America.

The recipe of Hayley Kiyoko's singular success as a queer artist? Her unique brand of reverie steeped in realism. Her gifts as a filmmaker cannot be overstated enough: clearly young Hayley was very attentive on the various sets she was part of since early childhood. Each of her songs and music videos takes a common experience of queer girls and elevates it, revealing Kyoko's deep understanding of the power of film.

Sonya's shawl dance for Coley to the backdrop of looming telephone towers on scorched yellow grass is filmed with the splendor of dance scenes like the famous vanishing ballroom sequence between Elizabeth Bennet and Mr. Darcy in the 2005 rendition of Pride and Prejudice, yet it operates within the very real ambiguity of female intimacy. To the outside, Sonya's boyfriend is witnessing Sonya's dance, too, albeit busy with striking baseballs into the sky. It stands to reason the dance may be for his benefit, which would cater to the wildly held belief that every action of a girl that might be deemed seductive MUST be meant for male enjoyment. But Sonya consciously dances under that shield of heteronormative assumptions with her fiery eyes pinned clearly on Coley who watches with rapture. Her dance invokes an image of ancient allegory as well: Salome's dance of the seven veils. It was Oscar Wilde who likened Salome's performance, originated from Mesopotamian myth, to the revelation of the unconscious: what the woman dancing truly veils and what she unveils, a secret known only to herself.

I had witnessed my own Salome's dance in my star-crossed college romance: the girl I loved having danced beneath the veil of cigarette smoke and fall leaves after I had encouraged her to pursue her passion for dance in the light of day. What started as a dare progressed to liberation and ended in a thinly veiled excuse for physical closeness that climaxed in a near kiss, ending abruptly when a female classmate walked in on us. My lover easily explained that Latin dances were passionate, her arms slung intimately around my neck. What was really happening may have been clear as day to her, to me, and even to the skeptical classmate of ours; but the time-honored equivocacy of female intimacy allowed all of us to linger in its shielding and stifling twilight.

Kyoko expertly explores this shadowy realm in her music videos, only to light-flood it with abandon: the seduction in Sonya's dance for Coley framed as undeniably blazing as the California sun above them. After Girls like Girls, dance would continue to manifest as Kyoko's preferred instrument to transcend the lesbian experience: be it as a dream sequence through a fantastical film projector in Sleepover, playing out a closeted girl's secret yearning for her friend, an outcast's defiant dance before a tribunal of High School Mean Girls in Gravel to Tempo, or in the dashing ensemble choreo in Curious answering the cruel games of a bicurious girl with stylish dignity.

All of these scenes might not strike straight audiences as anything profound: but to the queer audience it was representation and healing wrapped up in majestic dance routines that could have been lifted from the golden age of MTV. Moving and honest depictions of queer women's realities had scarcely been portrayed so boldly and optimistically, without obstructing the serious challenges of our minority.

Until 2015, like many young queer women, I felt like I had to be inscrutable. People were ready to declare me disgusting, sinful, and aggressive without ever having heard a word from my mouth; so publicly making a scene when a closeted or straight girl plays cruel games with you? Standing up to the mean girls that would make you out a freak for the mere fact that you were a little different? Beating up the sleazy and violent guy the girl you loved was with to desperately prove her straightness? Unthinkable. Through upbeat songs and music videos, Hayley Kiyoko told us: It's okay. You're allowed to show your pain. Your feelings are valid. You shouldn't be ashamed to dream and to want—and in the face of aversion and discrimination, you can not only proudly stand up for yourself, but joyfully dance in their face while looking absolutely fabulous.

Now the year is 2023. Hayley Kiyoko has just released a novelization of Girls like Girls to commemorate its eight-year anniversary. Its hardcover version comes with a book jacket depicting Coley and Sonya intimately huddled close, while the binding is merely stamped with the iconic yellow bike, so people in countries with no legal protection for queer people can read it safely by taking off the 'explicit' cover.

For it is 2023 and Uganda's president just signed a law that makes homosexual acts punishable by death. I still have never beaten up a homophobic assaulter and I don't plan to. Like people of all walks, I sometimes have a little projector going on in my mind like in Sleepover, showing both happy and sad memories of the girl I loved so long ago in that enchanted little college in Oregon. She was such a wonderful dancer, her intelligent eyes sparking gently when she talked about her passions and her dreams. I think she would adore Hayley's dancing and I still hope that one fine day she can watch it without fear or pain. One of the men who assaulted me in Colombia is in prison now. Unlike in 2015 I can now legally marry a woman in Germany. It is 2023... and Hayley Kiyoko powerfully dances onward, making beautiful reverie a reality with one subversive music video at a time.

****

A week after this was written Hayley Kiyoko's novel Girls like Girls became a #1 New York Times Bestseller.

Roxane Llanque

Can Yaman

It's been a long day. It would be awfully easy to fold like a pretzel into the couch to binge watch something on one of the many available streaming platforms, or get some dinner that will likely create a carbohydrate windfall, or have a glass of wine, some cheese, some chocolates... If only…

As the precious gap in my schedule opens, my thumbs fly along with my heart. My eyes wide in anticipation, butterflies in my stomach, dryness in my mouth, jittery legs, all the usual suspects join me in the insatiable craving for my fentanyl-free addiction. Let there be a new post. From you, from fan sites, anything to discharge the dopamine. It can be black and white or in color or even slightly blurry or edited poorly. I can understand why their hands might shake, I'm sure mine would too. My voracious eyes will block out all imperfections, eliminating those who surround and embrace you, for they will be envied later. Next time I'll take the time to study the picture, because I'm looking for an immediate fix now.

Six hundred Kettlebell-activated and Kegel muscles tense. A silent monk's paradise as the world around me freezes in eager anticipation as I scroll. And there it is. The breath you've kept prisoner, releases a tsunami against the pixels as your intoxicating, 2-dimensional image fills the screen and drowns every internal synapse in messaging. Like the Secret Service whisking the president away from an assassination attempt, my tunnel vision races your image to be safely ensconced into my subconscious. The caffeine of you coursing through my veins, a direct shot, nothing to process or ingest. You are with me. I tighten my laces. I can do this.

Gazing at the picture, an imaginary scent I've never smelled, sways the cilia involuntarily. Woody, fresh, maybe citrus, definitely spicy with notes of tobacco. I don't even like tobacco, but the momentary rush fills my face with a goofy smile that will be the "before Botox" picture- crinkles and wrinkles abound because of those dimples. My upper lip rises, and my teeth buck out as my broadly drawn cheeks stretch, reminiscent of the curling lips of the donkey smiling in Shrek. My euphoria squashing my usually rational state like peanuts in a grinder. You don't have to be smiling and our eyes don't have to meet, after all, I don't understand a word you say, and obviously we don't need to touch, since you are thousands of miles away, but you are more important to my getting healthy journey than the innumerable diets I've tried, the plethora of exercises I've experimented with or the medical health scares I've navigated. They were all important failed steps in my journey, that led me to you. The one who has inspired results.

Endorphins, Shmendorfins. I've never found exercise fun and it isn't from lack of trying a variety of things to find the one I enjoyed. Biking, spinning, swimming, walking, basketball, Pilates, barre, dance, weights. I've tried them all, hated the sweat, and like Elizabeth Taylor and her eight marriages, didn't stick with a single one. Yoga came the closest, but unlike the ease of folding like a pretzel onto the couch, yoga contorting was a lot a harder. Seeing your workout posts, how you push yourself even to exhaustion, I realized exercise may never be fun for me, but I have to find the motivation to do it. You feed that motivation.

There certainly is no shortage of good-looking celebrities who tout their exemplary physiques, using any opportunity to highlight their chiseled features. Of course, I've seen many who post themselves working out, but I've never been moved to move. Never heeded their call to action. All influencers have fallen on deaf ears until you. But you don't ask, you galvanize. Your contemplative confidence riding with carrier pigeons to reach me halfway around the globe. One of the earlier memories I have of you, in this never-ending journey toward habituating health, is a post you had doing pullups with a song playing by Kaleo. A line in there reverberates through my mind. "We get what we deserve." I can do this. I deserve more.

More what, one might ask? I live a purposeful life, filled with people who love and accept me as I am. People who understand when I don't come for a half day hike, because they know I find it too difficult and the recovery too arduous. People who love me with all the sagging bulges and bulbous flab that jiggles like Jello.

But there is more. Climbing up the stairs without being winded, getting up from the ground without a struggle, eliminating random headaches, avoiding the fatigue that plagues my existence. 'Health is wealth' the saying goes. Even with an emergency fund in the bank, I was body bankrupt. Your persona intervened, showing me the value of doing good for my body, so my body does good for me, now and in the long run. Now, because I'll never be at this moment again. I'll never get this moment back and what I choose to do with it creates a cascading effect, as I try to escape the genetic curse of my ancestors. In the future, so I'll be alive and well, unlike my own parents, to run around with my eventual grandchildren. I can do this. I owe it to myself to decide I am worth investing in, for all the mores.

How did you inspire this change in mindset? We are nothing alike, our differences are abundant: gender, culture, race, upbringing, siblings, foods, background, parents, schooling, athleticism, profession-none of them are shared. And it's not like others haven't tried to motivate through encouragement, invitation and sometimes, even shame. So what made you succeed where others didn't? Of course, one image of your broad shoulders and arms, where every muscle ripples like warm, poured chocolate curving through a fountain, is titillating. The defined contours of your silhouette are the definition of an Adonis. But your power over me comes from your eyes. Their intense energy exploding from the screen can change the course of the physical exertion of my day. Their soundless message

moving me from slug to spark, from couch potato to powerhouse. Decide you are worthy, they convey with their warm, deep brown color. Even beyond getting fit, you move me from dejected, rejected author, to courageous, tenacious writer. Without an utterance you motivate. Without being present you inspire. Your existence sparking ideas into motion and resurging outlooks to new highs. I can do this. It is my choice to do this.

People have said it before, but what you said in an interview stuck with me. Maybe it was your deep resonate voice, filled with the huskiness that still carries even if the foreign words are not understood. The translation wasn't very good, but you said something like, what you put in your body is your choice. What you do with your body is your choice, not the companies that make money off your poor choices. Love yourself enough to cherish the one body you've been given. No one else is going to respect your body for you.

Are you aware of the impact you have, your force of nature? Your eyes piercing my core. Your silliness curving my lips. Your acted sadness welling my lids. Your intensity vibrating my legs. Can you fathom the number of people who've watched your creative output and been lifted for a moment out of their numbness, out of their trauma, out of their loneliness? Those overcoming raging battles that can't be seen. Those taking a moment to rest before being strong for everyone else. Like sparklers at your ignition, sending waves of light in a multitude of directions, spreading like wildfire to withstand the onslaught of another day.

You must have an inkling from the droves that are present at your presence like pigs at the trough. Pushing, shoving, angling closer for a miniscule tidbit in the quest for unquenchable nourishment. As you scan the masses, person after person, selfie after selfie, autograph after autograph. You'll never know us. Our names running down in the whirlpool of a drain. But collectively, maybe the unnamed, undistinguishable energy feeds you. Isn't that what celebrity craves? Adoring fans that salute your ambassador brands, support your product endorsements, and consume your created, curated content. I hope we provide some small measure of joy. And I hope you have the non-trophy chaser people around you who allow you to be your truest self when you step away from the camera and the craziness.

As I work toward a better version of myself, as I devour social media to feed the hungry beast inside, I notice the uncivil and unkind words the mediocre spray your way. Do you have someone who picks you up during dragging durations? I wonder if you have one who touches you in inexplicable ways? As with every soul, a lot is perpetually asked of us from well-meaning family, friends and colleagues. The pressure to give of ourselves is weighty. Continually trying to attain greater heights, where simply being, is never enough. I hope when the monotony of your days presses down on you, you have a recourse. A source that lifts you without taking anything in return, because the comfort of your image pushes me to be consistent on my jagged path. You shine by example as I soar to the skies with my feet firmly planted on the sidewalk, step by step.

Despite all you've done for me, I do wonder…is this rational? Is this normal? Has my mania gone too far? Would I be able to tell if you became an impediment in my life, an obsession beyond the reasonable, where dereliction of daily duty was upended in search of you? Would I be able to extricate myself from this fixation, this compulsion, this infatuation? How can there be such an impassioned, visceral connection to someone I've never met? The women who follow you from city to city, is my fixation on the same level? What is it to be a fan? As a kid I wasn't the type that would hang posters on my walls or doodle names in hearts on my notebooks. As an adult, I regularly ridicule the phoniness of the celebrity culture. I shake my head at the people commenting on celebrity postings. My writings have shone a spotlight on how celebrity and the media push young girls to feel insecure. My poems We Fall Prey and Celebrity Nobody, mock our celebrity entrenched culture. What if you are a jerk in real life? Maybe you are the best actor around, seemingly intelligent, caring and giving, but masterfully deceptive? Am I insane to allow images to hold me in such a vice, where you've become the Helen of my Troy, knowing that I've believed myself to be above that fray before now?

Those are questions I don't have the answers to. I have no idea how long your hold over me will last. Likely it is a brief infatuation. The heavens collided to bring you into my life at the right moment after a medical scare. After all, people constantly come and go from our lives, leaving a bit of themselves behind like the doctors who helped me. You may not be there for the whole book. But however many chapters you are present for now, you've been a light drawing me in to believe in myself, that I can put in the work to achieve my dreams. Even if I don't see the bulges breaking down, even if progress is slower than I'd hoped, I know the changes you've kindled including daily exercise and veggie heavy meals have made me stronger, wiser and healthier. I'll never look like you (though from the back, the curl in our hair can look similar) and I'll never meet you (well…maybe I'll hold on to that dream), but because of you, I've taken ownership in my actions and I'm taking the essential steps toward my dream of a healthier me. I am a work in progress, a wellness warrior in your faithful army.

Thank you Can Yaman for your body of work, your body of love and your body of wellbeing. I'll be following.

D.S. Mohan

Music Saves Lives.

I understand the corny and cliché sentiments attached to the preceding sentence. Still, I know all too well the truth behind such a simple statement. Growing up in a constricting and quite aggravating social environment, music has always been an addictive yet necessary escape for me. Whether it is the old school R&B of the 1960's that my mother played around me, or the mainstream rock, hip-hop, and pop music I discovered as I came of age, listening to songs has painted numerous portraits for my overactive imagination to get lost in. Subsequently, there are multiple albums throughout my 35 years of life that define crucial periods of my time on Earth. Songs About Jane by the band Maroon 5 and Confessions by the iconic entertainer Usher are two significant examples of records which still inspire and uplift my soul. However, there is one defining body of music which has shown true staying power through my sweet triumphs and sour crises: Breakaway by singer-songwriter Kelly Clarkson.

Originally released in the fall of 2004, Breakaway is a dynamic sophomore record for Clarkson that has since cemented her status as a powerhouse in music. It followed her much publicized winning the first season of the reality television competition series American Idol, two years earlier. I can't recall the exact timeframe of my high school years when I bought the CD. What I do recall is that it quickly became a CD I played repeatedly. I also recall skipping zero tracks and drinking up all 12 songs each time as if they were bottled water for my ears. Given the struggles I faced as a socially awkward Black American millennial teenager boiling over with depression, anxiety and insecurity, Breakaway represents a saving grace that I strongly needed to get through the remainder of my teenage and young adult years. In a somewhat strange way, the lyrical angst and expression shown throughout the nearly 45-minute project resonates heavily with my own struggles, despite mine and Clarkson's differing backgrounds and life experiences. Perhaps that is why this is the project that makes me more of a fan of Clarkson's previous and subsequent works. Although my mother and I were impressed by her vocal talent and charming personality while watching her compete on American Idol, Breakaway unveils to me Clarkson's true abilities as a relatable storyteller through her music. Little did I know then how much this one album would aid me in a pivotal moment of my adult life.

Fast forward to the summer of 2014: I am a college graduate once again living in my childhood home with a degree in communications and no career whatsoever to show for it. I am employed at a window factory not far outside of my hometown. Because I am open to any labor experience at this point, I dive headfirst into this unfamiliar territory with an initially optimistic attitude—emphasis on the word "initially." As it turns out, cleaning and preparing windows for shipment is more challenging than one would expect. These tasks are even more daunting when the factory's work culture is outrageously toxic, filled with pessimistic supervisors, constant negative tension between coworkers, and broken promises of better labor experiences from upper management.

Although I make a positive impression among numerous coworkers and supervisors for my positivity and willingness to be a team player, the high product demand and increasing back orders result in 12-hour shifts from 8:00 am to 8:00 pm, seven days a week. Upper management tries throughout the following months to play around with the schedule to make labor easier for everyone involved. Unfortunately, upper management probably has a higher chance of solving the Rubik's Cube than fixing labor and scheduling issues. Throw in multiple coworkers either quitting or getting fired almost weekly, along with a cranky mentor who doesn't mind taking his personal issues out on me, and my positivity and team player attitude soon become heavily tested. How does someone get through a 12-hour work shift with poor company morale and a poorer sense of purpose? If you are me, you hum the entirety of one of the few albums you know by memory to make the day go by faster.

It is only a few weeks into working at the window factory that I begin to hum the entire Breakaway album, track-by-track, word-for-word, as each window comes down the assembly line for me to clean before the packers can wrap each one in plastic for shipping. Going over each song to myself dulls my sensitivity to the surrounding conflict and chaos within the factory. Soon enough, my overactive imagination becomes my savior when I envision both Kelly Clarkson and myself in imaginary vignettes inspired by the songs. The title track brings out my lifelong desire to see the world outside my hometown. From the hustle and bustle of a small-town factory to the harmonious beaches of Maui, I have "broken away" for just one moment in time. Perhaps the most gorgeously crafted song on the album, "Because of You" becomes a specific piece I love to hum during my work shifts and creates a specifically strong distraction during long days in a frustrating work environment. One of the more fun songs to hum, "Walk Away" is the smooth pop rock that I imagine singing to coworkers that rub me the wrong way, even though it's lyrically about a suitor unworthy of Clarkson's time. "Much like "Addicted," the penultimate song on the album "Hear Me" is eerie and urgent amusement that fits Clarkson's rockstar vocals perfectly. The final track on the record, a live performance recording of "Beautiful Disaster" from her debut album Thankful, is an exceptional way to end both the album and my own musical fantasy. While there may be other albums during this time I occasionally hum, track-by-track, word-for-word, Breakaway's presence in my mind and soul makes me feel that my circumstances at work and in life will improve.

Over the next four-and-a-half months, my labor in the window factory starts to wear on me as I watch peers come and go, sustain minor scrapes on my fingers and palms, and lose time with family, friends, and myself to a job that feels more damaging to my whole being with each shift. Eventually, I stand upon the belief that if they give me more to do than just cleaning windows, it will be more tolerable because stagnation makes situations like mine even more insufferable. Thankfully, the supervisors do offer me an opportunity to try painting some sets of windows. I feel fortunate for the chance to at least try my hand at a different task besides glass cleaning. In true fashion, my fortune becomes short-lived. One November evening, my supervisor asks me to go back to cleaning windows. He claims that no one on the current daytime shift can clean them as good as I can. Beyond disappointed, it is in that split moment I briefly hear Clarkson's voice, not in my ears, but in the stillness of my heart.

These lyrics from the first verse of "Breakaway" wash over my spirit in a way nothing has ever washed over me up to this point in my life. It is then, without hesitation, I give my supervisor the most profound "no" I have ever given to anyone up to this point in my life. When he asks if I am saying "no" to going back to cleaning windows or "no" to continuing at all as an employee at the factory, I know wholeheartedly that this is the perfect time to leave this place behind. After four-plus months of a torturous work environment, I decided to move on from a space which felt constricting and aggravating not just for my physical body, but for my emotional one as well. To my surprise, my supervisor and a few other coworkers take me to the bar and grille down the road to celebrate my departure out of respect for the hard work and positive attitude I showed throughout my tenure. Clarkson's words had empowered me to leave a life draining situation, an extraordinary moment I am only now soaking in as I finish this story.

Since leaving the window factory, I have uncovered jobs both at home and across the country that have been liberating and fulfilling. I genuinely cannot imagine what would have become of me if I agreed to stay at that factory, even if only for one more day. I cannot imagine my life without Kelly Clarkson and her musical endeavors, from her recent album releases such as 2023's Chemistry, to catching her perform on her daytime television talk show whenever I have free time. My greatest change since I left the window cleaning business is obtaining the emotional and mental stability I deserve. That fateful November night in 2014 has become the tip of the iceberg in discovering and nurturing my strengths. I do not write these words as a socially awkward Black American millennial teenager boiling over with depression, anxiety, and insecurity; I, too, am no longer constricted nor aggravated by my social environment. I embrace my unique eccentricities wherever my presence is needed. Gradually, my life has been saved numerous times because I am both compelled and encouraged to constantly break away, from inner demons, from victimhood, from unfulfilling and distressing places of employment… and therefore, my gratitude for Kelly endures.

D.J. Whisenant

Shirley Temple

My father sent me a birthday card once with the cheeky, smiling face of Shirley Temple on the front. I knew who Shirley was because sometimes her movies were shown on rainy weekend afternoons, probably aimed at the rest time of the retired or elderly, but lucky for me, I got to know the movies and stars of Hollywood's Golden Age. (An experience that informed my career path and fashion choices, but that's a story for another time.) I think I was about four when I got that card in the mail, and inside, my father told me he'd picked it out because little Shirley reminded him of me. I had brown curly hair and a big smile, but no dimple. Nor did I have exactly 52 little swirly ringlet curls from wearing rags in my hair overnight. I couldn't tap dance or sing either, but you know, parents are prone to these kinds of loving hyperboles when contemplating their offspring. (And rightly so.)

At four, I liked that Shirley could dance up a storm, had a sense of courage and adventure, and had loads of old-fashioned dresses with loads and loads of petticoats. (In reality those petticoats can be stiff and scratchy, but they sure are cute.) She was like a sweet little living doll, and in fact, doll versions of her were and remain highly collectible. I had the paper doll version at one point, cut out with scissors and showcasing outfits from some of her famous roles. I asked my mother about the rag curls that Shirley's mother famously put in her hair each night, and one day she did my hair in them for a ballet recital. The sectioned hair wrapped in rags are really uncomfortable to sleep in, I feel quite sorry for little girls who had to sleep in them regularly. They were kind of pointless in my case anyway, since I have naturally curly hair, but that's the kind of kid I was. (At one point, while reading Oliver Twist, I asked my mother if she could make me gruel for dinner so I could try it. I was a bit of an odd kid like that.)

The thing about Shirley Temple is that my mother didn't hate her. She hated Elvis. She hated Doris Day. She wasn't someone who was impressed by fame or hype at all, and she taught me, very wisely, that it's best not to look up to people, not to hero worship people or put them on a pedestal. People are only human, even the famous ones. Trusting your gut is better than blindly following a guru or idolizing someone. My mother hated anything saccharine sweet or that rang an overly cheerful false note. But she did not hate Shirley. Neither did my father, for that matter, and he was someone who really wasn't into frills or cutesy things at all.

Here's the thing. Shirley was the real deal.

Starting out at age three in 1931, Shirley Temple was a child star who was, like a lot of stars of the era, also able to sing and dance. She was in some really odd short films early in her career where all the cast were babies in nappies but were

doing grown up things like hanging out in saloons drinking milk instead of beer. (In that one, she was a saloon girl, it's oddly funny but probably shouldn't be.) She shot to fame with films like Bright Eyes, A Little Princess, Heidi…many of her films were about little girls who were taken in by emotionally damaged adults whose hearts she melted by reminding them of the child within, or stories where she remained hopeful and courageous in the face of bullying, mean-spirited adults and the hardest of hard times. She had a song in her heart and a dance in her step, which helped raise tired, lonely, defeated spirits. This was exactly the message that people needed in her era. My grandmother told me about how she remembered people knocking on the kitchen door to ask for odd jobs in exchange for food, and how they were starving. Her parents gave wholesome soup willingly to men who were out of work in this era, there was always a pot on the stove, and they took special care to make sure that those men weren't made to feel embarrassed or ashamed of needing help.

It wasn't their fault, it was truly desperate times.

This was the era when Shirley was the most famous, most recognized person in the world. The first really big, international star. She remained the biggest star in the world for over a decade. She was a huge celebrity. Huge. She was mobbed everywhere she went in the world, met heads of state and presidents, and was once gifted an elephant, which was a bit awkward. There were also some funny conspiracy theories about her, like that she was secretly bald and her hair was a wig, resulting in her having her hair pulled by random members of the public to see if it was real. And at one point the Vatican (for some reason, the Pope at the time was very concerned) sent out a representative to make sure she really was a little girl and not, as rumored, a really short adult.

The reason she really touched people was when she hit screens, it was the 1930's. WW1, at that time called The Great War, had changed battles from men fighting hand to hand, to massive, brutal deaths on a scale unknown before this time. Almost every family lost someone. Then the 20's had been a high time for some, but there was a lot of social change as well, which can be hard to process. And then there was the 30's. Shirley was the one bright spot in the Great Depression for many. It wasn't just because she was cute, and it wasn't even that her films were that good, necessarily. Some of them are better than others, but she was consistently great in them and always brought her A game. She was the face of innocence, the personification of playfulness and honesty in a world that was increasingly cynical, brutalized and felt dark and uncertain. Sound familiar? Some of her performances seem to show a calm gravity and a little wisdom beyond her years, too. People flocked to see her films, heading into the dark theatre to forget their troubles for a while.

Now, don't get me wrong, I'm not trying to convert you and I'm not a superfan of her movies, but I appreciate her work and what she did for people. As a phenomenon of fame, she is quite fascinating. And I know as you read this, you're rolling your eyes at me and you are saying to yourself, I bet Shirley was stuck up, or a brat or did drugs or something. Well, she didn't. Nor did she have some spectacular fall from grace or secretly hate a minority group. In fact, after she was (mostly) done acting in her early 20's, she went on to a career in philanthropy and diplomacy. She campaigned for children's rights, was on the board of the National Wildlife Federation, represented the US at the United Nations General Assembly, amongst other things, and was the US Ambassador to Ghana and Czechoslovakia at different times. She also had breast cancer in the 70's and by talking openly about it, not only raised awareness but helped reduce stigma. All of this in a time when a lot of women were only allowed to be housewives, generally speaking. She was a cool person and quite genuine and hardworking her whole life.

I read her autobiography last year after finding it second hand in the local library book sale. (It's called Child Star, it's good, if you're interested.) While reading it, it struck me that fame and celebrity were a bit different then. Though Miss Temple was a child actor, she really appealed to all ages. There were no ratings systems back then, it was all general admission, so anyone could and did see any film. Movies were aimed at audiences in a different way. So while a child star now would be marketed to children or maybe as a role model for kids, Shirley really was popular with adults and children of all ages. She was even loved by the guys in the military at the time and did some tours to meet the troops and boost morale. She was less of what we would now think of as an influencer, and more of a symbol or icon.

And this got me thinking. Right now, we're going through a time of turmoil and social change, a time when people often feel cynical and defeated, sometimes a bit hopeless or overwhelmed. Part of this, and our over-exposure to fame, is that we tend to be very suspicious of people who are squeaky clean or have a wholesome image, like she did. We see, not just big celebrities, but the smaller ones on YouTube, for example, aggressively marketing their personalities to sell products, or sell themselves as a product, and we are suspicious. People are seeing famous people and waiting for the other shoe to drop, assuming the successful are toxic in some way or hiding something. We look for evidence that they aren't so great, not so perfect. We look for how they got a hand up in life, what their privilege might be. People look for the catch and then they slide back into their shell, having proven once again to themselves that the world is a dark place and there's no use in fighting it. I don't think we would be impressed with a child star in the same way these days, and certainly not as broadly across the spectrum of demographics.

And yet, there's a deep interest in nostalgia at the moment, which I think in a way is the same impulse that Shirley Temple hit on. We want to look back to a simpler time, to a part of ourselves that believed, that was hopeful and brave. Innocent.

We're looking for the unspoiled self from our own childhood. We're looking for that simple heart that still believes it can stand up to the bullies and believes in happier endings.

I think most celebrities now are more into being a brand than a person (like Gwyneth Paltrow with Goop) or having a quippy, smart reply that's quotable and shows that they're on to what's really happening. The perfect comeback to the person on the other side of the fence. We think now that smart people are not cheerful, not happy. (Happiness is not cool.) Or even that happy people have no problems. Don't get me wrong, the Shirley Temple marketing machine was huge, but people now see themselves as a brand and identify with it. Shirley went to work every day and took her job seriously, and the marketing was done by the studio, and they made money off of it. Somehow, that little girl stayed grounded and did not buy into her own hype, and her genuineness hit people in the feels.

Saying all this, I am not even recommending a Shirley Temple movie to you. I'm not sure that I can. I think there may be something wrong with me, because after reading the biography, I was inspired to watch The Little Princess, because tiny me liked that movie, and I loved it all over again. I got emotional at the end, when her father finally returns and he doesn't remember her at first. And I went on to watch Heidi, and when (85-year-old spoiler) she's tricked and taken from her beloved grandfather, I felt really worried about her. And then a little later in the film, when her grandfather, a hard man who was avoided by the people in his village in the time before Heidi came to live with him, wanders the streets of the city to try and find his dear little granddaughter, and she's desperate to go back to him, well, maybe I did get a tear in my eye. It could be childhood nostalgia or something, but I do feel good after watching her films. They're funny and sweet and they really work to make you feel something good. A little more hopeful, a little kinder, maybe. And you know what? I'm not a cool person. Part of me is an eternal child who gets delighted by the small things. I'm not blind to the things going on in the world right now, not at all. I get worried and anxious. And I am cynical about celebrities or people who are human marketing machines. But, (and I know this isn't a cool thing to say) I also believe that bullies get theirs in the end and a light heart and a little kindness, a little playfulness, go a long way. Or that the simple things count. And while a song can't fix your problems, it doesn't make them worse.

If Shirley Temple graced the big screen today, she wouldn't have the same impact. We are too changed, as a world and as a society. We would want to see the receipts. We would have strong ideas about who was allowed to like her and people would bully other people who didn't fit that definition of who could be her fan. It would be considered cool not to like her. And maybe that's kind of sad. I mean, celebrity isn't everything, but imagine being alive in that era and sitting in a cinema where one of her films were playing. Imagine how almost everyone in that cinema would have lost someone in the war, like your family had, or that this movie ticket was a huge treat you could barely afford and the stranger next to you could probably barely afford. The people in the cinema would have different political views, different backgrounds, different jobs, but all of you would be hit in the heart in the same way, and maybe share a smile, maybe be a little easier in your mind or show a little more kindness because you all watched a little girl be brave and kind and sing a little catchy tune. And maybe you laughed at the same places or cried at the same parts. It's kind of amazing that she brought people together the way she did.

Well, to bring it back full circle for you, my grandmother was a little girl in Shirley Temple's era, and she told me that when she was little, she desperately wanted a dimple like Shirley, so each night she went to sleep with one finger poked into her cheek, in the hope that when she woke up, it would have created a little dimple. It didn't work.

Hermione Flavia

My Celebrity: Mary Ann Csipkay-Stadler

In the late 1970's in Indiana, I held my mom's wooden tennis racket with my small hands, marking the start of my love for tennis. I will never forget the weight of the racquet as I grasped it firmly, determinedly dragging it along while positioning myself in front of the television, trying my best to emulate the poised players of the US Open. The rhythmic thud of the ball against the strings, the noises that would pulsate from the players during tense moments, and the intense emotions displayed by the winners on screen fueled my young imagination, planting the seeds of a passion for competition. I dreamed of playing at the collegiate level.

I began my trek at ten years old by playing competitive tennis tournaments across Indiana, Illinois, and Ohio. My mother was my coach, and she would spend endless hours with me on the court in preparation for upcoming tournaments where I faced opponents with the best coaches and equipment that money could buy. I, on the other hand, was graced with grit and modest determination. Throughout the years, I searched the newspapers for information about the women's tennis team at Indiana State University, a university approximately 35 minutes from home. One season, as I was flipping to the Sports Section of the Tribune-Star, I noticed a newcomer. Mary Ann Csipkay was a top recruit from New Jersey, and she came onto the scene ready to win. I followed her and read the newspaper articles about her—she was a force. I was drawn to the words writers would craft about her on-the-court demeanor, that of a fierce competitor. As I reflected on myself, my beliefs fluctuated about whether I could achieve my dream of success by securing a tennis scholarship at a Division I university, just like she did. Nonetheless, I continued to work, winning and occasionally losing while continually dreaming of playing at Indiana State University, just like Mary Ann Csipkay.

Before I knew it, her four-year tennis career had concluded, and she was gone from the newspapers; I often wondered where she went after graduation. I missed reading about her, and while I continued to watch the Women's Sycamores, my passion for the team was a little more subdued. And then, in 1992, I couldn't believe my eyes as I read the Sports Section. Much to my surprise, Mary Ann had been named the Head Coach for the Women's Sycamore Tennis Team. Soon after being named the Head Coach, I watched her play a competitive match. It was one thing when I read about her being on the court, but seeing her in person was a completely different experience. I was a sophomore in high school then, and I knew I had to play for her, on her team; only then would my athletic dreams be achieved.

I won tournaments and gained momentum as my ranking climbed. I became one of the top players in the Indiana Girls 18 & Under Division. I began receiving offers to play tennis on scholarship; I couldn't believe it. Was my dream coming true? Not yet, because I hadn't caught the eye of Coach Stadler. Yes, there is a name change because, during this time, she married the love of her life, Henry Stadler IV, who was an incredible individual in his own right. I had to get her attention somehow, but I didn't know how. Then, my time to shine was upon me. I heard through the grapevine that she would attend one of my matches, and I knew it was a now-or-never moment to impress her. I remember the match like yesterday, although it was around three decades ago. I vividly remember how I had laid my heart on the court and lost. Looking back, I knew I could have won—I choked. I watched her walk away and thought, well, I blew it; my opportunity to play for her was over.

Emotions flooded my mind. In the landscape of my formative years, the concept of celebrity diverted from the glitz and glam of Hollywood; instead, it manifested in the rhythmic thump of tennis balls bouncing on the court. Coach Stadler was an amazingly talented coach and an accomplished player in her own right. As an ISU alum, she held many records I could only have imagined achieving. She had the most remarkable presence and the best smile that would penetrate a room; people noticed and respected her. Not only was she a coach, she was a successful player, and I deeply respected her for that. Other coaches I would meet with knew the game and could coach the game, but were not players. I wanted to work with someone who could be on both sides of the net: a coach and a player. I had been in her presence but could never work up the nerve to approach her to start a conversation. And now it would never happen.

Then, one afternoon, a few weeks after my debilitating loss, the phone rang, and I answered; remember, this was the pre-caller-ID era. To my disbelief, it was Coach Stadler. She had called me! She told me she had followed my career and thought I would be a fantastic asset to her Sycamore team. What? I couldn't speak! I must have finally said "YES"; honestly, I do not recall. And so my college-level athletic career began. She was a mentor wielding a deadly racquet and a frequently unreturnable forehand, a mentor for other mentors to learn from. As I traversed the country's tennis courts, her coaching expertise transformed her into a guiding light. I played tennis for her for four wonderful years and accomplished what I suspect was more than she could have dreamed for me; it undoubtedly exceeded my expectations. I passed one of her school records and ended my career with 100 career single wins. I only lost a few singles matches over four years, and she was always there cheering me on whether I was winning or found myself behind…never wavering, never giving up with a smile that I vibrantly recall today. Beyond being a symbol of tennis prowess, she evolved into a compass, steering me through my tumultuous college years and beyond. She was there when I needed someone to talk to about relationships off the court. She could help me see the right way without appearing condescending, and I continued to gravitate to her for guidance. The distance between coach and athlete dissolved as time passed, and a true friendship blossomed, transcending the confines of the court. In her, I discovered not just a coach but a confidante, morphing into the sister I never had. A bond established through a mutual love for the game solidified with a lifelong respect for one another.

Once, over sushi, we laughed as she realized she had been pregnant for most of my collegiate career, as she had three children during that time. She was mom to three boys with whom she was endlessly in love. As our conversation continued over sushi that evening, I remembered one of her pregnancies and how we would be taking a trip to play tennis some 600 miles away, and she never wavered. I asked her how she did it, and she said, "It was easy; I did it for you girls. You meant the world to me." I smiled and felt her genuine love and respect for her team. During this dinner, I also opened up about how I never thought I would have been able to play for her, and I was nervous being around her at the beginning of my career. She thought this was very funny and didn't honestly believe me. As we left the restaurant, we hugged, said our goodbyes, and thought about when and where we would meet next, heavily contemplating another sushi outing.

We did not have another sushi dinner or any other get-together. Tragically, one fateful Easter morning in 2005, I received the call that a drunk driver had shattered her magnificent life into irreversible fragments. Daughter, wife, mother… my coach, my friend, and my sister figure were abruptly taken away, never to be seen again, gone, unbelievably too soon; she was 38. The news struck with the impact of a meteor, plunging a deafening silence into my court of life. I couldn't play tennis after the news of her passing. Over time, I realized that avoiding the court probably wasn't her preference for me. She would have encouraged me to persist in playing.

I miss her. I would have loved watching her soak up every moment of her husband and boys and their successes. I miss her life advice. I wish she could have met my husband and my children; I wish I could have witnessed her reaction to my motherhood. I always wanted her to coach my kids the way she coached me. I will do my best to fill in for her as their liaison to the tennis world.

Navigating the labyrinth of grief prompted me to contemplate the intricate interplay between personal connections and the influence and evolution of a public figure's relationship. Though not a traditional celebrity, her impact resonates in crucial choices and the defining aspects of my adulthood. Our connection evolved from a prominent figure to a supportive coach on the sidelines, shaping my narrative and transforming into a bond that extends beyond the tennis court into transcendent dimensions.

Lyndee Phillips

Love Don't Hate (It Might Make America Great): A Journey with James Baldwin

The year was 1987. I would have been a college sophomore had my family not imploded, forcing me to take an unexpected "gap year" in Baltimore, Maryland, to manage the fallout of my father's most recent relapse. Our family had just relocated to Baltimore from a sheltered, lily-white suburb of Cleveland, Ohio. I remember my understanding of race was mostly a patchwork of awkward family conversations and sanitized prep school history lessons. I was singularly unprepared to meet and interact with my father's new neighbors (mostly black and brown folks) who resided in the dilapidated row house he now called home. I scrambled to find a job—with little more than a high school diploma and a smattering of freshman level college courses—to help cobble together a new family income from meager savings and disability checks.

A couple weeks into my new job as a law librarian's aide (aka the Xerox gal), I stumbled upon James Baldwin's The Fire Next Time at my favorite (now sadly defunct) book seller, Louie's Bookstore Cafe. The bookstore was conveniently located on my walk home from work, and the owners were surprisingly tolerant of my pseudo-vagrancy, allowing me to browse for hours on end as long as I bought a cup of coffee and didn't hold up a table during the lunch rush. The book's cover was unremarkable—your standard author's picture coupled with some assertive, blocky font—but there was something about Baldwin's expression: a mask of stoicism straining under the weight of rage, frustration, hope, and love, that sparked my curiosity. Little did I know that the book would be so pivotal to my self-development. His words grew like persistent weeds transforming the carefully manicured lawn of my suburban identity into something much less controlled, and ultimately more satisfying.

Baldwin was a black man, a writer, a thinker, and self-declared exile within his own country, when not a de facto Parisian expat fleeing the daily grind of racial hostility in 1960's America. His voice—both in writing and speaking—was a potent mix of anger and eloquence. He spoke of a racial chasm so vast that it felt more like a canyon carved across the American landscape than the all too visible line that divided the so-called "good" part of town from the "bad."

"You think your pain and heartbreak are unprecedented in the history of the world, but then you read," Baldwin observed, "It was books that taught me that the things that tormented me most were the things that connected me with all the people who were alive, who had ever been alive." No doubt, my initial contact with Baldwin was through the lens of my supersized self-pity and panic over my failing family fortunes; fortunately, true to his word, the power of Baldwin's writing slowly nudged me off the safe ledge of naive complacency and self-absorption, allowing me, for the first time, to peer into the abyss of American race relations in all its complexity, and consider and connect with the pain of others.

This encounter was not—and is not—comfortable. How could it be? Baldwin made it abundantly clear in his 1965 debate with the white conservative thinker, William F. Buckley, that he believed that "the American Dream is at the expense of the Negro." Baldwin declared in this same debate, "I picked the cotton, I carried it to the market, and I built the railroads under someone else's whip for nothing." His indictment was clear: Blacks provided the "cheap labor" that built the foundations upon which the freedom and prosperity of the white middle-class American family now resided.

Amid the ongoing "culture wars," it may be hard to appreciate the raw originality of Baldwin's injunction against white Americans, a testament to how his work has shaped a new generation of anti-racist scholar-activists like Ibrahm Kendi, Robin DiAngelo, and Eduardo Bonilla-Silva. These scholars have successfully adopted and adapted many of Baldwin's core insights and converted them into the conversational currency that now in turn fuels anti-woke memes, TikTok, and talk radio. The question remains if they have done so in a way that honors the skill, complexity, authenticity, and hope of Baldwin's work.

Baldwin was a vocal critic of "the collection of myths to which white Americans cling"—myths like we were/are living in a colorblind society, or blacks and whites share the same optimism that the police serve to protect them, or the judicial system to defend them. His words provided guidance to black readers actively negotiating the white narcissism and racist gaslighting that was pervasive in the 60's and 70's. They also powerfully called for introspection among his white readership to confront some hard truths about the white cultural tendency toward violence, and the delusional narratives we have sometimes concocted to excuse them. Baldwin's work requires the death of white innocence.

I remember experiencing moments of anger and indignation reading Baldwin that day at Louie's Bookstore and Cafe, and feeling unfairly implicated in a system I hadn't actively or intentionally built. But the force of Baldwin's words made it hard to remain in defensive denialism or innocence for long. He seemed less interested in assigning blame or cultivating guilt than in delivering a clear-eyed diagnosis of the problem and in offering a solution: love. The elimination of racism not only requires the death of white innocence, but also the death of black rage. In a remarkable, open letter to his nephew, Baldwin entreats him to accept—even love—the white racist. "There is no reason for you to try to become like white people," Baldwin writes, "and there is no basis whatever for their impertinent assumption that they must accept you." Instead, he continues, "the terrible thing, old buddy, is that you must accept them. And I mean that very seriously. You must accept them and accept them with love…They are, in effect, still trapped in a history that they do not understand, and until they understand it, they cannot be released."

Baldwin's call for black Americans to accept and even accept with love white Americans –even active racists –will likely seem outrageous and unrealistic, especially in an age where social media platforms like TikTok and X have become breeding grounds for content that further exacerbate racial tensions. However, any discussion of The Fire Next Time that overlooks this aspect of Baldwin's work is missing something important. Baldwin's appeal to love is not anomalous or incidental, but central to his daring and original definition of integration, and fulfillment of an authentic version of the American Dream. He wrote:

"If the word integration means anything, this is what it means: that we, with love, shall force our brothers to see themselves as they are, to cease fleeing from reality and begin to change it…and we can make America what America must become."

These words forced me to confront how my life, my very identity, was shaped by the accidents of history and birth. Before reading the book, my primary concerns narrowly revolved around the financial anxieties impacting my (still) middle-class family. Baldwin's work required that I extend my scope of concern to consider how my circumstances were intertwined with the condition of others. "The paradox of education is precisely this—that as one begins to become conscious, one begins to examine the society in which he is being educated," wrote Baldwin. This certainly was the case for me; his work required consistent and focused attention to address the deficiencies of what I came to see as my narrow, if expensive, education in American social realities and to begin to imagine what an education that worked to promote the American Dream for all would look like. I credit Baldwin's work in no small part for rekindling my desire and drive to return to college and complete my degree in Philosophy, develop my interest in public philosophy and community engagement, and become involved in the Inside-Out Prison Exchange.

While Baldwin did not attend to (at least not to my knowledge) the racist undercurrents of the American prison system and the long-lasting effects that mass incarceration has had on black American families, Baldwin's call for integration and love continues to inspire a new generation of educators and students engage in programs like the Inside-Out Prison Exchange that seek to foster dialogue and empathy between incarcerated individuals and college students across profound social differences. This unique educational program brings these two groups together for semester-long courses held within prisons. Through shared learning and discussion, participants challenge preconceived notions about crime and justice, race and class and other forms of social division, fostering a deeper understanding of one another's experiences. This process requires hard work and a willingness to ask Baldwin phrased it, "take off the masks we fear we cannot live

without and know we cannot live within," shedding the mask of white superiority, and the mask of black rage. It requires us to try and try again to open communication—especially when it sometimes feels futile or impossible. It is in this way we begin slowly to dismantle stereotypes, empowering both "outside" students and incarcerated "inside" students to together imagine and work towards a more just system.

The Inside-Out Prison Exchange Program's emphasis on human connection and mutual respect is the closest thing I have ever experienced to a truly integrated and loving classroom, which of course, is ironic given the fact that class takes place inside a level four (intensive) security prison.

It is in Baldwin's call for love and integration that the true power of his work resides, distinguishing it from the work of many recent anti-racist scholars, like that of Robin DiAngelo, who often seem more focused on cultivating white guilt and black rage, than on finding a way forward through the exacting work of love. This is not to say that Baldwin wasn't angry, or that his writing sought to suppress or censor black rage. Baldwin acknowledged, "To be a Negro in this country and to be relatively conscious is to be in a rage almost all the time."

Yet, Baldwin understood that lasting change wouldn't be achieved either through black rage or white complacency. Love, for Baldwin, serves as the bridge across the racial chasm by requiring all Americans regardless of race, color, class or creed to engage in the "tough and universal sense of quest and daring and growth." The work demands deep empathy, a recognition of our shared humanity, to foster true connection required to dismantle the systems of oppression that impede our growth as fully functioning and free individuals. By advocating for love, Baldwin offered a more radical and ultimately more hopeful vision for racial healing, a vision that compels us to move beyond self-righteous indignation and defensive posturing, to choose the difficult, yet transformative, path of love and together work to "end the racial nightmare, and achieve our country, and change the history of the world."

Ashley Geiger

Ani

I sat in my online meditation group on a Thursday morning in February. This group made up of people from all over the country met every day at 7:30am California time, where the host lived. They were a constant source of comfort. They listened as I battled myself, showing fatigue and attempting to quiet obsessive thoughts around a recent betrayal. I had a big painful thing I was carrying around with me now. It was given to me by two people who made a decision to pursue a drawn-out, selfish, and destructive impulse, made possible by proximity, convenience, and unstable spiritual ground. They teamed up for one short season to burden me with a wound that cut to my soul.

An addiction had developed to poking at my pain around the betrayal. Like mouth pain. When you can't stop messing with a sore tooth or running your tongue over a spot on your gums that stings. I couldn't keep my mind away from visualizing physical acts or imagining intimate conversations that exposed my family to an unprincipled interloper. I insisted on knowing the gory details, demanding to hear at what exact moment he took off his wedding ring. He tried not to tell me but finally exploded that it was while she was lying in his lap. I had badgered him into admission. What's your poison?

I repeatedly interrogated. Making him tell me everything and hoping each time, he would say something that lessened the impact of the bludgeoning. I latched onto words like "empty" and "hollow." "Juvenile" and "junior high." Anything to reassure me that our love and life were real and that whatever just happened was only a devastating symptom of a shared illness we needed to treat together. In sickness and in health, indeed.

My heart was broken in innumerable pieces and something in my lizard brain was telling me that to put it back together and protect myself from it ever happening again, I would need to understand and intellectualize a thing I couldn't change.

No matter how much I tried to think it away, this thing happened and my job now was to get about the business of healing. A large job. A very fucking large job that doesn't happen in the head, I was told. It happens in the heart.

Every one of my meditating friends on this daily call that sometimes I make it to and sometimes I don't, is an admitted recovering addict. Most of us have quit a substance or two. As I described my compulsion to return over and over to dark and painful thoughts, hoping they might go away if I just thought them real good one more time, they all nodded knowingly from their West Coast Zoom boxes. They chimed in about that one drink they could always justify. Or that one hit of whatever it was that would surely be the very last. I continued to wonder aloud what my brain could possibly believe was beneficial about returning again and again to the imaginings that made me want to throw up or caused actual pain in my heart. What was the reward? If I do it this one last time. This will make the pain stop.

We finished our 7-minute meditation designed to last 20 minutes but because they held space for me and my shit this morning, we sat for 7 minutes. No one begrudged the abbreviated sit. We were all happy for the silence in any amount. We came back and our teacher asked us how it was. One friend said it was a good "reprieve." The word, "reprieve" means to delay a punishment. A death sentence is reprieved. Relief is offered. Respite from suffering. A break from pain or trouble.

Reprieve is Ani Difranco's fifteenth studio-recorded album out of a total of 23. It is very chill compared to her other work, particularly the albums before and after it. It makes me wonder what was going on with her when she wrote and recorded it. The marketing materials accompanying the release my favorite record store owners held for me were her own drawings of trees and birds. Natural browns and greens. Was she offering or receiving the rest that comes after an arduous healing or being held accountable for something?

It came out in 2006. I was working for an advocacy agency offering services to legal victims of Domestic Violence in the Toledo Municipal Court. I had just met my eventual best friend when we hung identical Ani Difranco posters over our desks in the office. We would go on to "jump ship and swim" and start an Independent Advocacy agency together. This would be the first of many agencies or businesses I started from a need to work outside of dysfunctional systems. Always an independent advocate. And always with Ani as the soundtrack.

This advocate friend awakened my feminism and taught me how not to be afraid of the word or the act of identifying as such.

A break from being punished solely for being a woman. At least that's how I understand it. As in the cancellation of the punishment of Eve. Do we ever get to stop looking at women as temptation and sin? Are women allowed to concern ourselves with things other than being attractive but not too attractive to men? Is it ok for me to not be a "pretty girl"? Don't I have more important things to do?

In 2016, in November specifically, I got real, real mad. And so did you, if you were paying attention. It didn't go away. It made me resent men's power and devalue their contributions out of bitterness. The most qualified person in history lost the Presidential election to a white supremacist slob monster. The ramifications were many and varied. This anger began to warp my relationship with one very important man. My husband. It would take until after the big painful thing to realize my extreme and one-sided participation in the world had done some serious damage. You can't love and live with a man whose opinion you aren't giving its due weight and consideration. You can't have a happy marriage with a person whose mind and ideas you aren't paying attention to anymore. Or that you are rejecting. When it truly is his mind and the way he sees the world that you love about him. That you always have. There were growing hints this dynamic was not sustainable. I was defensive and frustrated. He was distant and brooding.

Ani Difranco released at least one if not more albums every year from 1990 until 2006 when she became a mother two times over. From 2008 - 2012 she did not release any studio albums. I read once where she said her children considered her guitar competition for her attention and that she was scarcely allowed to pick it up until they were in kindergarten. I wonder if she resigned easily to those years without work output. I know I didn't. Two years? Ok. But, three? Four?

I panicked. I didn't know who I was anymore. I knew I had more to offer the world than being a mom. I met so many obstacles in my pursuit to reintroduce myself to the professional world, my confidence was on the ropes. I was jealous of my husband's outward successes and experiences because, behind the scenes, I was becoming dangerously invisible. To us both. I was crucial to keep our world spinning but my personhood was being ignored, undermined, and taken for granted. The uphill and slow climb to actual professional achievements of my own had extra obstacles in the form of strife at home and begging for support and dependability. The hurt was taking root and became another avenue for an iteration of my feminism. I tapped further into Ani's penchant for pointing out the absurdity of paternalistic God figures. How is literal creation not listed in the column under "woman"? Ummm…. We make babies. When do we get the credit for that? Ever? Is anyone paying attention? Don't you want our perspective? We know stuff about how to do stuff. Humans eat from our boobs.

Ani went from writing about asshole boyfriends to writing about babies. She shares poignant theories about menstrual cycles and the idea that women mourn every egg that doesn't become a child. She paints something in mysticism that we usually chalk up to hormones. She reminds us and inspires us to think about women as divine creators.

She talks about softening and choosing peace. But, that doesn't stop her from boldly taking on reproductive rights or the scourge on humanity that is the United States of America because you can be an activist outside of the home and take care of your family with warmth and nurturing. Both and all are necessary.

She matches her ambition with her softness the way women of different generations advise me to do as I balance and integrate the masculine and the feminine within myself and my household. Ani can write poems about her abortions and

about being a mother. She can write hopeful songs about Crocuses at the end of winter and pursue programs to bring an end to capital punishment. She integrates receptivity with assertiveness. I co-authored a book about taking down a sexual harasser and sent it along with a traveling musician friend who recently signed on Righteous Babes Records. Lilli Lewis and I met when I opened for her at a Roe v. Wade music and poetry event at Toledo's Collingwood Arts Center. She has pledged to put the book in Ani's hands when the time is right as they both live in New Orleans. It is my offering to Ani's request that feminists don't sit back and let her do all the work. That we see our individual purpose and do something with it.

During my healing from the big painful thing, my Independent Advocate friend and I went on an overnight trip to Ann Arbor. We stayed in a hotel with a pool and a hot tub, went swimming twice, ate good food, drank champagne offered upon arrival, played cards, and listened to only Ani Difranco. Reprieve was the first album that defined our friendship. It was gentle and supportive and still very badass. Just like us to each other. We listened to it as we developed programs to improve our community's response to domestic violence in 2007. And we listened to it as she beat me in Rummy over chocolate-covered strawberries and baklava in 2024.

We talked about being over stimulated by our families and our jobs. We talked about grieving. She permitted me to feel my feelings and not to try to rush a process that had no timeline. We talked about meaningful rest. We acknowledged the reprieve the weekend offered us both.

I went home feeling fresh and ready to embrace joyful moments with my family. We played frisbee in the big field and had morning dance parties before school. It lasted a few days. Until it was time to think about the painful thing again. This time in the context of shared resources and debt. Until someone suggested there was something I could have done to stop the painful thing from happening. I reminded myself and the person who suggested it that I did try to stop it, and couldn't. It existed as an entity. This painful thing. It had a life of its own. Its life devastated my life but I didn't get to control it. Especially not in hindsight.

Ani's hindsight is a gift she provides to me because her maturity sinks in as she puts sing-able lyrics and a singular musical sound around it all. She crafts songs that become mantras. They are heartbreakingly lilting or they rock your face off. She delivers her wisdom half a decade in advance of my same or similar evolutionary step. Ideally, she helps me to distill complicated feelings down to a line or two.

I craved the reprieve I achieved from the previous weekend. I wanted it back. But,

I had returned to the rehash. The dissecting and berating. I made him answer more questions. His answers about feeling numb enough to do it and conflicted enough to follow through with additional humiliation tied to the public nature and documentation of their affair didn't cut it in my midnight rage. I wanted still a different explanation. Something that erased her. But that was impossible. I didn't know how to get the peace back. I was afraid I never would. I knew that healing and grief happen in waves but tell that to the wave while it's happening. It doesn't listen.

I was invited to see Hadestown in Dayton during my healing. Ani Difranco originated the role of Persephone when Anaïs Mitchell recorded the first concept album in 2010. The piece traveled for over a decade on its way to Broadway and eventually won 9 Tony Awards including Best Musical in 2019. I followed and fangirled over its every move. Ani is playing Persephone on Broadway at the time of this writing. I wish I could afford tickets and the trip to New York City. Karmic lives show those full circles if we devote ourselves to evolution.

Ani started as a dancer before she wrote songs. Persephone and Hades share a dance that is the point I can count on crying every time I see the show. A surprising and sweet waltz. Disarming and pure. Ani introduced us all to Anaïs Mitchell and offered me another muse when she released her first albums on Righteous Babes Records.

I talked with my theater date about the idea of reprieve and she suggested that to stay in peace I might do well to notice and acknowledge the small reprieves so that they may grow into larger ones. I came home again to a morning rainstorm that seemed to be washing away as much of the residual pain sludge as I was willing to release. All of it, please. Take it all.

I came home to sweetness but woke up angry again. I wanted to involve all the people involved in my pain. I still wanted them to hurt like I was hurting.

My morning was consumed by a need to tell her grown son about it. Her son who was conveniently hired to work alongside my husband with tools and opportunities for bonding while the adulterers stole glances and moments together. She was given fodder to picture their future as a couple or even a family. She fabricated a delusion that she could edge me out of the actual life he and I built together. He said things to her like, "This isn't right. I need to try to salvage my marriage." And she said things to him like, "Well, we can't go back now." She insisted that all signs and synchronicities pointed her toward him and their future. He communicated misgivings and tried to ease his way out, attempting to preserve the friendship he had ruined by initiating this mess. She put on the full-court press. A text from her, "I love to watch you work," was my first clue to the entire affair.

While they were "at work," our daughter and I were "at home." Even our child was powerless to stop what was happening with her 7-year-old intuition. "Is Daddy cheating on you with her?" my little baby, who was about to grow up too fast, asked me. I wanted to send her son a message. Did you know about your mom and my husband? How our home was full of tears while the two of them were naked together in her studio? The studio you and he worked in together. Did you know how she laughed when she told me about their sex and how she didn't seem to think it was that big a deal? "I feel for you and your daughter," she said to me, using our child's name with a familiarity that set me on furious fire. Oh, you do? What specific feeling can you identify? I'm very curious.

Before the big painful thing, I had hired this woman on jobs and supported her work for years. Our kids played together while we collaborated on projects. We went to her daughter's birthday party.

I wanted to ask her son how that made him feel about his mom. What about his mentor who he thought was like this super cool family man? Ask him if he had time to get his daughter a birthday gift last year or take her to the doctor with pneumonia when I was out of town or if he was too preoccupied with "work" and your mom. I found her son online and began to write the message as my husband and I got ready for our newly energized morning walking routine. It wasn't the first of its kind. Part of my addiction was telling everyone what they did. To expose the hypocrisy that carried the insult to my injury. He imposed religious law dictating a pause in the intimacy inside our marital home but it didn't apply when he was with her. He declared us celibate but could find his way to fucking her. Wanting to tell her son felt awful. But, it was that sick kind of satisfaction I had been pursuing. It was picking at a scab or stitch. I was still trying to bleed out the pain. How, though, could I live in hard-earned peace with my husband that morning, and quietly do something hurtful to this young man at the same time?

I let the craving pass like I did with cigarettes until I finally quit. I didn't send the message. I chose a different kind of satisfaction. Not the fast heart pounding, the sweating and shaking I had become accustomed to since the day I learned about it all. The bodily reactions got me prescribed an anti-itching medication that doubles for anxiety and sleeplessness. The pill bottle my husband is nervous to have around because of my ideations. I convinced myself she'd have to tell her son herself someday. When he asks why they don't work together anymore. She'll have to come up with some answer. And that's her problem. Not mine. If I can keep making those kinds of decisions, not to poke the pain, peace will surely follow. And in longer stretches.

My husband and I returned home from our walk and used a broom and shovel to urge the water out of our flooding driveway and down into the flooding street.

"Water seeks its level," he always says. Even when the Earth is sinking into itself in front of the garage.

Parallel in timing to the big painful thing, I was offered a part in a show, a one-woman show about a kid with a suicidal mother. The thing was written for me. It had elements of Jazz and a love for record albums. It talked about emotional abandonment and neglect. It felt like a timely deep dive into parts of myself that might help me process some major things once and for all and be able to bring an audience along with me–every performer's dream. To hold an audience in your hand as you usher them through a series of emotions. Much like any Ani Difranco concert, which has been described by Anais Mitchell as they toured together as "transcendent." Never not a spiritual experience. You always leave changed. And I would know, I've lost count of the number of times and venues where I've seen her live.

She talks about how her voice shows up from day to day and that's what the recording or the audience gets. She doesn't overthink the way she sounds. She expresses what she has that day in that moment. Her songs sound different every time because she is a different person every time she performs them. Even different from the person who wrote them.

After the big painful thing, I took another route. I decided to, as much as possible, cultivate joy. I quit the show and set down the inconvenient timing and the tediousness of memorizing and rehearsing a one-woman show about suicide.

After the big painful thing, I took back my name. I kept it when I got married thinking I was taking some kind of stand. But, I let myself down by not using it when it counted. Ani has always been a Righteous Babe and Righteous Babes Records has always been Ani. She has rehabbed buildings in her hometown, signed artists, and launched careers. She is a leader in her industry and has always and will always do things exactly how she wants to. She is all sides of my feminism, even the ones neither of us has discovered yet. Even the blind spots and the sometimes ignorant whiteness. Even the mistakes and the admitting of mistakes.

Just like Joni Mitchell did with the 60-something-year-old song "Both Sides Now," Ani has created the timelessness and perspective that comes with growing into a new woman every day. All on the back and the fingers of this tiny mighty musician who toured with her self-recorded and produced album, "Educated Guess" with a broken ankle and a guitar just to keep her tour team in work.

I never even looked up the meaning of "reprieve" until 18 years after the album came out. I didn't need to know exactly what it meant. A break, yes. Rest, sure. But, specifically, a stay of punishment. Mine. His. Hers. Theirs. As much as I have wanted everyone to hurt as I have because of the big painful thing, peace is worth the end to this addiction. I fought for my family and myself and I and we won. We are whole and I am seeing, allowing, and acknowledging the reprieve. I want the big painful thing to have not happened. But, it did. In my meditation group that sometimes I make it to and sometimes I don't, our teacher says, "It's like this." And it is.

Rachel Richardson

A Eulogy for Dr. Heathclifford Huxtable…from a Cosby Kid.
(1937 - 2018)

When I was younger, long before I lost my own flesh and Dad, I frequently wondered how I'd hold up…the day Bill Cosby died. I even confessed to my brother, Rasheed, that it just might be the saddest day of my life. For someone who, at the time, still had both birth parents under one roof … it seemed to stop just credibly short of hyperbolic. For a kid, a Cosby kid, whose saddest day up to that point had been "that one time our rabbit, Button Nose, escaped and I tried to catch it with a Louisville Slugger that bloodied its nose." What can I say? It's hard being eight years old.

By 1986, Cliff Huxtable, MD, had become a Thursday Night, backlit floor unit fixture in American homes for no less than two years since its first episode in 1984. Then, no one could predict how Orwellian the brownstone at "10 Stigwood Avenue in Brooklyn Heights" would become. In hindsight, someone older than me should have placed the facade of the private residence that served as the "Cosby Crib" in Greenwich Village, Manhattan. Cinematography is often sleight of hand. Nothing personal. However, the illusion doesn't end there.

A year later in 1987, approaching the apex of its eight-year run, The Cosby Show aired episode 12 of Season 4. Titled "The Locker Room," oddly not for the kind of talk that Cosby's comedy worked tirelessly to avoid, the episode's rundown would ultimately prove more ominous than the slug.

Summary: Theo tries to prevent Vanessa from dating his friend Lyle. Cliff wants to know how Rudy's magic tricks work.

Juxtaposed with the storyline of Cliff's only surviving male heir (Theo) attempting to protect his teen sister (Vanessa) from dating his classmate who "chases women," is the storyline of the "The Great Rudini." Somewhere between eight and nine years old by Season Four, *Rudith Lillian "Rudy" Huxtable* is the youngest of the Huxtable children. By the time Episode 12 comes around, she becomes infatuated with magic…like most children her age.

Clair (Cliff's wife and mother to all five Cosby Kids…including Rudy): Are you ready to perform feats of magic, oh Great Rudini?

Rudini: Yes, I'm ready. I hold in my hand an ordinary drinking glass.

Cliff: … *somehow clapping too soon after an awkward and pregnant pause*

Clair: Please, hold your applause until the end.

Rudini: My assistant will pour milk into the glass. Momina, the milk.

Clair (AKA "Momina") Pours milk

Rudini *as "Momina" pours*: … Thank you. Ladies and gentlemen, isn't she beautiful?

Cliff: … *somehow cannot clap soon enough, while suggestively raising both eyebrows in accord after giving Momina a quick once-over*

"Momina": Are you going to drink the milk, oh Great Rudini?

Rudini: No. I am going to make it disappear.

Cliff *pipes in incredulously*: Impossible!

Rudini: You shall see, oh doubtful one! I shall now say the magic words. Abracadabra. Hocus Pocus. Make this milk go out of focus.

Scene.

****

Dr. Heathcliff Huxtable was much more of an "art imitates life" kind of guy than vice versa. A Dad's Dad in every sense of the word. A Rorschach inkblot of a dad bod in a Koos van den Akker sweater. In striking contrast to the polyester-cotton blend of unicolor jumpsuits customarily adorned by Black men in America should they live long enough. In fact, at the height of America's "incarceration complex" in 2001, the likelihood of a Black men spending time behind bars in their lifetime was 1 in 3, while it was 1 in 17 for all U.S. men. The kind of folk Cliff's doppelganger, Bill Cosby, referred to as "backwards."

Bill Cosby (from his "Pound Cake" speech at the NAACP Legal Defense Fund awards ceremony in 2004): People putting their clothes on backwards. Isn't that a sign of something going on wrong? Are you not paying attention? People with their hat on backwards, pants down around the crack. Isn't that a sign of something or are you waiting for Jesus to pull his pants up? Isn't it a sign of something when she's got her dress all the way up to the crack—and got all kinds of needles and things going through her body. What part of Africa did this come from? We are not Africans. Those people are not Africans; they don't know a damned thing about Africa. With names like Shaniqua, Shaligua, Mohammed and all that crap and all of them are in jail.

Dr. Huxtable was different. An enigmatic codex to refashioning our future selves, the old fashioned way. Sweaters designed to provide a contrast from the other characters on screen. Taped in front of a live studio audience, the Cosby Show would shoot every episode twice. More than just a modern day skin, the sweaters helped facilitate the magic of television. According to Show costume designer Sarah Lemire, "We ended up doing close-ups of (Cosby) so you could cut between the first and second show. The sweater became an easy way to control that."

Bill ("Pound Cake" continued): But these people, the ones up here in the balcony, fought so hard. Looking at the incarcerated, these are not political criminals. These are people going around stealing Coca-Cola. People getting shot in the back of the head over a piece of pound cake! And then we all run out and are outraged, "The cops shouldn't have shot him." What the hell was he doing with the pound cake in his hand? I wanted a piece of pound cake just as bad as anybody else, and I looked at it and I had no money. And something called parenting said, "If you get caught with it you're going to embarrass your mother." Not "You're going to get your butt kicked." No. "You're going to embarrass your family."

Dr. Huxtable was always in control, even when playing the heel. Surely an accomplished OB/GYN, a "miracle of life whisperer," could figure out his pre-adolescent daughter's magic trick. But he didn't, because that wouldn't be funny. Heathcliff Huxtable became a naval officer just to prove that Black folk could swim. Lost a brother, James Theodore, just to prove we could survive loss without losing ourselves. Played football and ran track, just to prove he was fast, Black and could take a beating. He even wrestled, to show us that Black people could succeed in non-Black spaces. Went to Meharry, the only real life, private, historically Black medical school in the country. He blurred the lines between what we could dream…and what we could become. If only for one Thursday a week.

Bill ("Pound Cake" continued): Five or six different children—same woman, eight, ten different husbands or whatever. Pretty soon you're going to have to have DNA cards so you can tell who you're making love to. You don't know who this is. It might be your grandmother. I'm telling you, they're young enough. Hey, you have a baby when you're twelve. Your baby turns thirteen and has a baby, how old are you? Huh? Grandmother. By the time you're twelve, you could have sex with your grandmother, you keep those numbers coming. I'm just predicting. [...] What is it with young girls getting after some girl who wants to still remain a virgin. Who are these sick black people and where did they come from and why haven't they been parented to shut up? To go up to girls and try to get a club where "you are nobody…." This is a sickness, ladies and gentlemen, and we are not paying attention to these children. These are children. They don't know anything. They don't have anything. They're homeless people. All they know how to do is beg. And you give it to them, trying to win their friendship. And what are

they good for? And then they stand there in an orange suit and you drop to your knees: "He didn't do anything. He didn't do anything." Yes, he did do it. And you need to have an orange suit on, too.

****

Oftentimes, as artists, we harness our gifts to create versions of ourselves that we desire to be. When we are successful, other people believe it. Ask most any gangsta rapper you know, Bill. As much as Bill Cosby became "America's Dad," the Shaniquas, Shaliguas, and Afenis had Tupac Amaru Shakur…America's son.

Tupac: "I might just be my mother's child, but in all reality, I'm everybody's child. Nobody raised me. I was raised in this society. I am a society's child. This is how they made me, and now I'm sayin' what's on my mind and they don't want that. This is what you made me, America."

The question we are left with, in the wake of Dr. Heathclifford Huxtable, is not whether he was right about all the Tupacs of the world, but whether the monster created Dr. Frankenstein or Dr. Frankenstein created the monster. Some say Pac took the role of Bishop in the movie Juice and never came back. Perhaps, for eight seasons, Bill desperately tried to become Heathcliff … but he couldn't shake himself.

Dr. Heathclifford Huxtable was born to be a deliverer of sorts. More gynecologist than anesthesiologist at the outset. Somehow, Bill got more into chemistry than chivalry. A different kind of Black magic. The kind where even The Great Rudini's glass of disappearing milk is not safe…if she doesn't disappear it fast enough.

They will never cry for Cosby, as I did for Cliff in 1992. Gawker's Tom Scocca said, "nobody wanted to live in a world where Bill Cosby was a sexual predator." Especially in a world where, as Salon's Brittney Cooper put it, "We are not a society given to slaying our patriarchs." And welp, every patriarch has a penis.

They say history repeats itself. But what if it is the future that repeats itself… and what we continually experience is simply a syndication. A rerun, where the only notable differences are the commercials. In the 30 plus years since the final episode of The Cosby Show aired, the distance between the greenroom couch and the broken fourth wall has evaporated. A reckoning that Dr. Huxtable conveniently side-stepped by taking his final curtain at the show's end in 1992. Three months younger than Cosby himself, Heathcliff definitely presented more Libra than Scorpio. Either way, he is survived by a constellation of childhoods that will always remember that he and Bill Cosby got canceled for different reasons.

Hakim Bellamy

In Search of Mexicans in Hollywood

I've never liked the story of the crabs in the bucket, how a crab can't get out or get to the top because the other crabs will always bring it down. I don't like that story as it applies to Mexicans, how we don't support one another, how we bring each other down.

Erik Estrada was the first brown-skinned man I ever saw on television, the first in a starring role. He played Frank "Ponch" Poncherello on CHiPs. His character's full name was Francis Llewelyn Poncherello.

> Poncherello is not a Hispanic surname.
> Mexicans do not name their children Llewelyn.

It turns out the show's creators had envisioned the character as an Italian named Poncherelli. Erik Estrada, with a few acting credits already under his belt, asked if the character—a positive role model—might be Hispanic. And so it was that Poncherelli became Poncherello.

> Poncherelli, apparently, is not an Italian surname.
> Prior to CHiPs, Estrada's acting credits included a pimp and a drug dealer.

Erik, born Henry Enrique Estrada in East Harlem, New York, resurfaced in the 90s on the Mexican telenovela "Dos Mujeres, Un Camino." Torn between two women, he was the camino, so to speak.

> Much was made of Estrada's accent. Like me, he didn't grow up speaking Spanish. Like me, he learned as an adult. Unlike me, he learned for a television role.
> I learned because I felt a part of me was missing.

Maybe Erik Estrada was not the first. Maybe it was Luís and María on Sesame Street with their brown people names and brown people lives. Sometimes they spoke Spanish. Agua, el número cuatro, hola, vamos.

Luís and María weren't their real names. I didn't know until decades later that he was Emilio Delgado and she was Sonya Manzano. I didn't know until years after their deaths that my paternal grandparents, Paul and Rosie, were really Pantaleón and Rosaura.

Luís proudly declared on an episode of Sesame Street, "Both my parents were born in Mexico, so that makes me Mexican-American." I never saw that episode when I was a kid.

> Though, even if I had, I would have thought of myself differently. My parents

were not born in Mexico. My grandparents were not born in Mexico. My mother's paternal grandfather was born in San Luís Potosí, her paternal grandmother in Texas. Her maternal grandparents were born in New Mexico Territory. On my father's side, my great grandparents were also born in New Mexico Territory. With the exception of Crecencio Moran, my great grandparents didn't come to this country. They stayed in the same place, and the country to which they belonged—or tried so hard to belong—changed around them.

Luís owned the Fix-It Shop.

I knew by the hands of the men in my family that Mexicans could fix things.

Sonia Manzano and Erik Estrada are Puerto Rican. I didn't know that there were different kinds of brown people, that a María or an Estrada could be something other than Mexican.

The US Border Patrol categorizes immigrants who are not from Mexico as OTM, or "other than Mexican."

Emilio Delgado was born in Calexico, California and grew up in his grandparents' house in Mexicali, Baja California, México. Calexico and Mexicali are sister cities whose names are what Wikipedia describes as "a portmanteau composed of Mexico and California."

I would describe many people I grew up with as a portmanteau of Mexico and New Mexico, something that could only exist along the US/Mexico border. In my lifetime, my own family has been more New Mexico than Mexico—born on this side of the border, English-speaking, Spanish lost with our parents' generation, who were punished for speaking it in school.

In 1987, when I was fifteen years old, Linda Ronstadt released Canciones de mi Padre, a traditional, Spanish-language mariachi album. As a musical guest on Saturday Night Live, she sang vestida de charro, with a Mariachi Vargas de Tecalitlán backing her. Harp, guitarrón, trumpets, Mexican men in sombreros. She sang Los Laureles and La Cigarra. I could hum along, but I didn't know the words.

I was looking for us and hiding from us at the same time. I was something not quite Mexican. "What are we?" I once asked my older brother. We weren't white. We weren't Black. We didn't speak Spanish, so we weren't Mexican. We ate enchiladas and menudo and beans and tortillas. We tanned easily. He answered, "We are Americans of Hispanic descent."

Maybe the crabs are protecting one another. It stands to reason that if you're at

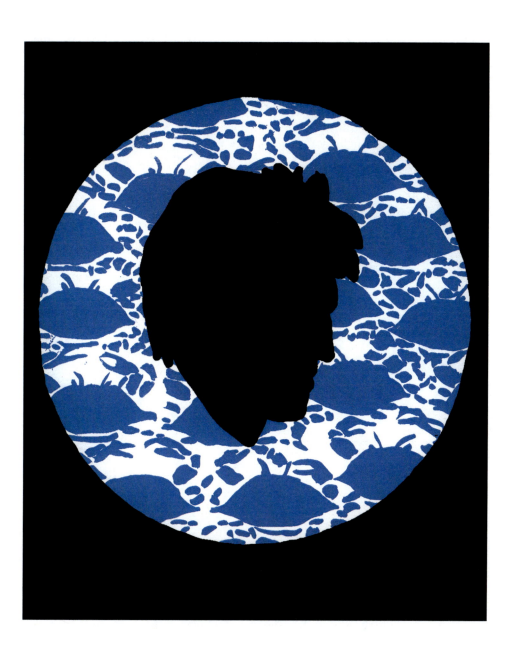

the top of the bucket, you'll be first in the pot.

Spanish actress and musician Charo was also a fixture of late 1970s/early 80s television. She busted out of her tops, wore tight pants. Her main dialogue in appearances on The Love Boat, Fantasy Island, and Hollywood Squares was, *Cuchi cuchi.*

To be fair, this was also the title of her first album. In my house, thirty miles north of the US/Mexico border, we never used the phrase *cuchi cuchi.* Not a single brown-skinned person in my school or town ever said *cuchi cuchi*—unless we were quoting Charo. Her tight clothes, thick accent, and hip shaking embarrassed my mom. We don't talk like that.

Charo's full name is María Rosario Pilar Martínez Molina Baeza. She was—and is—an internationally-acclaimed flamenco guitarist.

What I wish my mom had asked while we watched those episodes of Love Boat: See what we have to do to be famous?

Maybe humans and crabs are different.

Lucy, you've got some 'splaining to do.
Arriba, arriba.
Ay, ay, ay, ay, oh I am the Frito Bandito… You sing the Frito Bandito song, and you're loco for crunchy Fritos corn chips.
Te adoro, Anton.

My friend Adolfo insisted Natalie Wood was Latina.
She wasn't.

I want to live in America.
Smiles, everyone. Smiles.
Are you pulling our noses?
Sí, mi jefe.
Would you say there is a plethora?
Chico and the Man
Freddie Prinze
AKA Pablo
The George Lopez Show
Madonna plays Evita in the film adaptation.

Madonna is not Latina.

Cómo la flor

Estoy muy excited.
Jennifer López plays Selena in the biopic.

                                        Did Cindy Crawford really criticize J-Lo's butt?

Freddie Prinze took his own life in 1977.
Selena was shot and killed by the president of her fan club in 1995.

      All these years later, I still miss her, still wonder what she'd be singing now.
Jane the Virgin: Gina Rodriguez, Jaime Camil, Andrea Navedo, Yara Martinez, Diane Guerrero, Justina Machado, Ivonne Coll, Rosario Dawson, Rita Moreno in one show!
Like my grandmother, Jane the Virgin's grandmother spoke to Jane in Spanish. Like me when I was a girl, Jane answered in English.

Charo made a cameo on Jane the Virgin. She played Recuerdos del Alhambra on guitar. She talked to Larry King about what that moment meant to her. "It was an answer to destroy the image of *cuchi cuchi*."

And then Gina Rodriguez had to tweet that Summer, 2017, in response to promotion of Black Panther, Marvel's first film centering a black protagonist: "Marvel and DC are killing it in inclusion and women, but where are the Latinos?! Asking for a friend…"

Sigh.

                            Maybe crabs and humans aren't so different after all.

                                                      Michelle Otero

Contributor Biographies

Roshelle Amundson is an Associate Teaching Professor of Writing, English, and Humanities at The University of Wisconsin-Green Bay. She is truly passionate about teaching, writing and communications, and using our voices to speak for those who cannot. In her spare time, Roshelle may be found refueling in the quiet; gardening, foraging in the woods, or walking the shores of Lake Superior or Lake Michigan—her pockets full of rocks and fossils.

Hakim Bellamy is the Inaugural Poet Laureate of Albuquerque (2012-2014), a two-time National Poetry Slam Champion (2005 and 2006) and past Creative Writing Chair at New Mexico School for the Arts. His poetry has been published on the Albuquerque Convention Center, on the outside of a library, in inner-city buses, and in numerous anthologies across the globe. Bellamy was recognized as an honorable mention for the University of New Mexico Paul Bartlett Ré Peace Prize for his work as a community organizer and journalist in 2007 and later awarded the Career Achievement Award for the same Prize in 2018. In 2017 he was named a Kennedy Center Citizen Artist Fellow and previously served as the on-air television host for New Mexico PBS's ¡COLORES! program for three years. Prior to pursuing a law degree at the University of New Mexico School of Law, Bellamy served as deputy director for the City of Albuquerque Department of Arts and Culture from 2018 to 2022.

Erin Boyle is a multimedia artist living in Chicago. Through her poetry, creative nonfiction, and collage she explores themes of interpersonal connection, music, romanticism, sincerity, and politics. She is currently finishing her undergraduate degree in English with a concentration in Literature at the University of Illinois at Chicago. Erin plays cello in the University orchestra and organizes with the Chicago chapter of Students for a Democratic Society. She is the winner of the University's Paul Carroll Creative Writing Award.

Coe Colette is a queer, non-binary artist, writer, musician, and mixed-media creator who has lived a thousand lives in their 30 years. Drawing inspiration from their real experiences, Coe's work explores the weirdest corners of the human psyche. In their essay, Coe confronts the tumultuous midlife crisis that engulfs them at the age of thirty. Far from the glamorous vision they had imagined, this crisis is a collective period of mourning, fueled by years of suppressing sorrow.

Hermione Flavia is a writer, cinema journalist and book reviewer, who studied movie history and film making in Australia, before attending the film school at Ealing Studios in London. She started covering preview screenings there, as well as working in the independent film scene, winning some awards for her screenplay writing. She now lives in Canada with her cat Grimoire, where she makes her own vintage inspired clothes and rides horses.

Ashley Gieger is an Associate Professor of Philosophy at the University of Toledo, where she focuses on public philosophy and community-engaged arts. She has been involved with the Inside-Out Prison Exchange Program since 2016 and was named a Marc Sanders Media Fellow for 2024-2025. She lives on a small homestead farm with her partner Tim, three turkeys, two goats, two pigs, two ducks, two dogs, and twenty chickens.

Laureli Ivanoff is an Inupiaq and Yup'ik writer who cuts fish and makes seal oil in her home community of Unalakleet, Alaska. She believes the land is sovereign and thanks settlers for coffee.

Roxane Llanque is a queer writer and filmmaker of Bolivian ancestry. Her award-winning short film Aberration was featured at the Madrid Human Rights Festival and her story The Tell-Tale Present won the 2023 OutStanding Miniature of World Pride Australia. Her writing has appeared in Libertine and is forthcoming in Flint Magazine. She's based in Berlin, where you can find her cheerfully playing wistful Spanish songs on her guitar or on Twitter @roxanellanque.

John Mauk began public life as rock musician, then devolved into a rhetorical theorist with a penchant for epistemology. Later, he took up literary writing. His fiction has appeared in journals such as Salamander, Arts and Letters, New Millennium Writings, The Forge Literary Review; his nonfiction in Rumpus, Beatrice.com, and Writer's Digest. He has two full-length story collections, Field Notes for the Earthbound (2014) and Where All Things Flatten (forthcoming 2024). He also hosts a YouTube video series, Prose from the Underground, which features interviews and craft talks for working writers.

D.S. Mohan's writings explore the need to question our beliefs on what has always been. Trying, every day, to bypass the mindless pitfalls established to sidetrack people from staying informed and grounded in what is truly important, she's focused on continuing difficult discussions. A firm believer that each of us has a story to tell, and it behooves us to tell it, because no one else will do it for us, she strives to live her life with peace, passion and purpose. Her work has been published with Fairfield Scribes, Brown Girl Magazine and Yellow Arrow Publishing. Connect with her on Twitter @mohan_shuba and Instagram @timetoriz

Michelle Otero is the author of Malinche's Daughter, an essay collection based on her work with women survivors of domestic violence and sexual assault in Oaxaca, Mexico as a Fulbright Fellow; Bosque: Poems (University of New Mexico Press, 2021), a collection written during her tenure as Albuquerque Poet Laureate; and her memoir Vessels (FlowerSong Press, 2023). She is a member of the Macondo Writers Workshop. Originally from Deming, New Mexico, Michelle holds a B.A. in History from Harvard University and an MFA in Creative Writing from Vermont College.

Lyndee Phillips currently resides in the great state of Michigan, but she is a proud Hoosier hailing from southwest Indiana. Sports were also a big part of her Indiana upbringing as she played basketball, baseball, golf, softball, and volleyball, with a special place in her heart for tennis. After earning her Bachelor of Science in Management Information Systems from Indiana State University, she dove headfirst into international business consulting, with a soft spot for the picturesque Zug, Switzerland. She earned a Master of Professional Studies in Organization Development and Change from Penn State, and is currently working towards a Doctor of Philosophy in Organizational Leadership. Her research focuses on cardiac practitioners' perceptions of integrating artificial intelligence into cardiac-enhanced recovery after surgery programs. She lives with her husband, two children and three dogs.

Rachel Richardson is a veteran jazz and folk singer, guitarist, published author, cultural event and public art coordinator, and all-around performer. She is a lifelong community activist. As a professional advocate for victims of domestic violence, she co-founded Independent Advocates in 2007, which produced a Court Watch Report in 2011 recommending a Domestic Violence Court in Lucas County. As the founder and CEO of Art Corner Toledo (ACT), she has coordinated over 60 murals in downtown Toledo and surrounding neighborhoods. Rachel holds a Bachelor of Arts in Interdisciplinary Studies focusing on Sociology, Ethnic Studies, and Non-Profit Management from the University of Toledo. Under her business, Rachel Richardson Productions, she and her family co-wrote and illustrated Just Worms for Dinner in 2020, a children's book and call to arms to collect worms for Donald Trump to eat in prison. She co-authored On Drowning Rats: How Two Women Took Down a Sexual Harasser and How You Can, Too with Cami Roth Szirotnyak. She was a longtime columnist for the Toledo Free Press Star, published in Death Never Dies (2021), an award-winning anthology edited by Lee Fearnside, and SWELL Magazine. She hosts programming at Jazz Alley in Toledo's Glass City Center. Rachel is a product of Toledo, Ohio, and mom to Naima, wife to Yusuf.

Sandra Rivers-Gill is a native of Ohio. She is an award-winning poet. Her work has been featured in numerous journals and anthologies, and she is a Pushcart Prize and Best of the Net nominee. Sandra is a teaching artist and mentor, and serves as a judge for poetry competitions. Her debut chapbook, As We Cover Ourselves With Light was published by Sheila-Na-Gig Editions (2023). Visit her at https://linktr.ee/sandrariversgill.

Emma Snyder (she/her) is a writer, a crisis counselor, a member of the LGBTQ+ community, and the co-founder and editor-in-chief of Tabula Rasa Review. She is dedicated to writing about mental illness and healing until she or the character feels better; either or. You can find her work in The Emerson Review, Abstract Elephant Magazine, Periphery, The Magazine, The Abbey Review, and Furrow Magazine.

Most people can pinpoint a celebrity who was their "sexual awakening." For Emma, it was a "bisexual" awakening, and Marilyn Monroe was hers. Around the time she turned 16, quintessential posters of male celebrity crushes were replaced by pin-ups of Marilyn in all her glory, blonde curls resigned to black and white print. She bought hundreds of Marilyn Monroe collector's cards (who knew those were a thing??) and carried them to college with her, adorning her dormitory with her portraits. Emma was still in denial about her sexuality then, joking with her roommate that she was very much straight, but Marilyn was the exception. Years later, when Emma came to terms with being bisexual and what that means for her, she stopped joking that Marilyn started it all and began to mean it.

Robin Stock is a career fundraiser, communicator and strategist. By day, she raises money to support research, access and equity in the higher education sector. Her side hustle as a ghostwriter of romance novels has allowed her to see more than two-dozen of her stories in publication. She is an avid rock hunter, voracious reader, enthusiastic lover of music, sports and food, and an unapologetic Marvel nerd. She lives in Perrysburg, Ohio and counts among her favorite people her husband, Jesse, and children, Alia and London.

D.J. Whisenant is a poet and an essayist under the name D.J.W. A 2011 graduate of Tiffin University, his writing has appeared in books such as O! Relentless Death! and California's Emerging Writers: An Anthology of Nonfiction. His poetry can be found on WordPress.com through the title D.J.W.: Words and Sounds. In addition to writing, he also works in home healthcare, tending to elderly, disabled, and health-compromised individuals in need of assistance. D.J. enjoys listening to music, traveling, daydreaming, and learning about how to be his authentic self. He currently resides in Youngstown, OH.

Jennie Young is an English professor and writer in Green Bay, Wisconsin, where she directs the Writing Foundations program at UWGB. She publishes in humor, education, feminism, and rhetorical theory; her work can be seen in McSweeney's, Ms. Magazine, The Independent, Inside Higher Ed, HuffPost, and elsewhere.